Volume One

Pingshan Mantis Celebration

5 Volumes
10 Years Ongoing Research

China Southern
Praying Mantis Kungfu Survey™

Volume 2
China Mantis Reunion

Volume 3
Kwongsai / Iron Ox Interviews

Volume 4
On Monk Som Dot's Trail

Volume 5
Chu Gar Mantis Celebrations

Also available!
5 volumes in one multimedia eBook!

坪山 螳螂 慶祝活動

Pingshan Mantis Celebration

35th Anniversary of

Wong Yuk Kong's
Kwongsai Bamboo Forest Temple
Praying Mantis Kungfu

by

Roger D. Hagood

Charles Alan Clemens, Editor

Southern Mantis Press | Pingshan Town, China

Southern Mantis Press
462 W. Virginia St. (Rt. 14)
Crystal Lake, Illinois 60014
1-800-Jook Lum
books@southernmantispress.com

Ordering Information:
Special discounts are available for martial art schools, bookstores, specialty shops, museums and events. Contact the publisher at the address above.

About the cover: Top to bottom images are the late Wong Yuk Kong and his sons, Wong Yu Hua and Wong Yao Hong.

ISBN: 978-0-9857240-0-9

Dedication

Sifu Wong Yu Hua and Wife

I have never met a better example of a gentleman Sifu, in China. Wong Yu Hua is well respected in kungfu circles throughout South China and Hong Kong. He is down to earth, unpretentious, and considerate of others. I am grateful to him and his family for his long friendship. --- RDH

Monk Som Dot's Ancestral Shrine

Kwongsai Jook Lum Temple
Praying Mantis Kungfu

Hoc Yurn; Hoc Yi; Hoc Kungfu

學仁 學義 學功夫

Jurn Jow; Jurn Si; Jurn Gow Do

尊祖 尊師 尊道義

Respect the Ancestors for their transmission of the art.

Respect the Sifu for his teaching.

Respect the Older Brothers for their dedication and loyalty.

Respect the Younger Brothers for determination in training.

Contents

Preface

It had been some time, since I had last visited Wong Yu Hua , Sifu, in Pingshan Town, Guangdong, China, when in 2002, I returned to his large four storey gated home, unannounced.

I asked my assistant, Mr. Lam, to ring the bell for the third floor, three times. The answer from the intercom was "what do you want?" to which the reply was from Mr. Lam, "I am here to see Sifu Wong Yu Hua."

After a pause, the reply was "Wong Yu Hua has gone to Beijing and will not return for one month, Sorry."

So, I rang the bell again myself and said in my best Chinese, "his friend has come from the USA to visit and is downstairs."

The gate was buzzed open and Wong Sifu greeted me warmly. We had a jovial and friendly reunion. We had not shared company since 1992.

I later found out, that the first reply was due to the fact that, unless it was urgent, Wong Sifu no longer opened his medical clinic, although, many people still rang the bell regularly seeking various treatments.

Over the last 10 years Wong Sifu and I have explored up and down the East River all three branches of Monk Som Dot's Southern Praying Mantis Kungfu. The result is this 5 Volume Survey. I'm thankful for Yu Hua's graciousness and grateful for his strong keen interest in Southern Praying Mantis. In this, we are like minded.

RDH

Pingshan Town, Guangdong, China

Summer, 2012

Intent - Warrior Spirit The first principle is intent or will-power. Intent is simply defined as the "warrior spirit." Without it, there is no focus of the body and mind into one purpose. Strike with the soul, and you will never miss. Thought and action are one.

Pingshan – the Hometown of Jook Lum Temple Mantis

Pingshan Town, Longgang District, Shenzhen City

Since 1976, I've lived in China and Asia more than 20 years. In 2002, I returned to mainland China to further research the origins, history and practice of Southern Praying Mantis Kungfu. Little did I know then, where that quest would take me. Some ten years later now, I'm still living in Pingshan Town, Guangdong Province.

Pingshan is a bustling town that some consider a village. Actually, it's a non-stop, 24 hours a day, metropolis, comprised of some 125 smaller villages, most of them industrial. In 2004, it was put on the map by the opening of the first McDonalds' franchise.

35th Anniversary Celebration of Wong Yuk Kong's Kwongsai Mantis

The closest Kentucky Fried Chicken is still 20 minutes away, but, I expect someone is looking to open a franchise here soon, especially, since, in all of the province, the local chickens are noted for their tasty meat and unique features of "three yellow spots and a beard," that is, yellow beak, yellow feathers, yellow feet and red beard. **Update 2012**: Pingshan now has two McDonald's and a KFC, although Pizza Hut is still 20 minutes drive away.

Pingshan is located in the Longgang District of Shenzhen City, east Guangdong province. Guangdong Province is situated in the southern most part of China and has a population of some one hundred million people comprised of 42 individual ethnic

Pingshan Town is only a 52 mile swim to Hong Kong!

Images following are all from the Pingshan Mantis Celebration!

groups, one being the Hakka people. Very fertile, with as little as 15% of it's land under cultivation, the province still produces twice the national average of rice.

Legend states that the capital city of the province, Guangzhou, was founded by five celestial beings who landed from the sky riding on the backs of five flying goats, each with a rice stem in it's mouth. The five gods, wishing this area to be forever famine free, gave the ability to grow rice to the local peasants.

After the beings departed, the goats turned to stone. In 1959, Guangzhou paid tribute to these benevolent goats and erected a granite statue in Yiexiu Park, Central district, as the city's symbol. Today, there are many "goat statues" in the "Goat City", but perhaps, Yiexiu park has the most impressive.

Longgang—the Dragon Hill District

Established January 1993, Longgang District is a municipality of Shenzhen City (some say the next Hong Kong). The area has a history of more than 600 years and exceptional geographic advantages. Early settlements along the coastline were fortresses

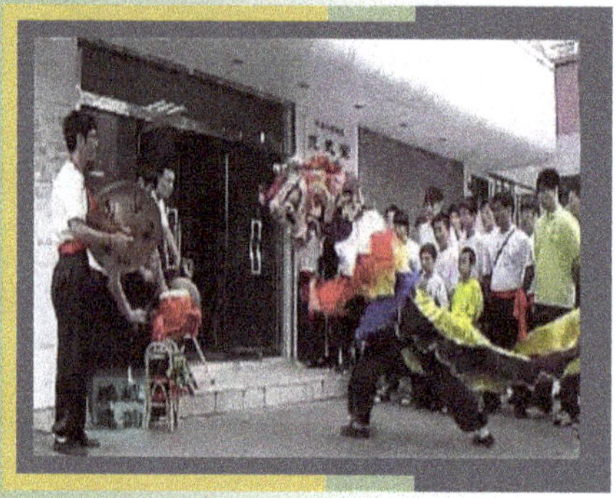

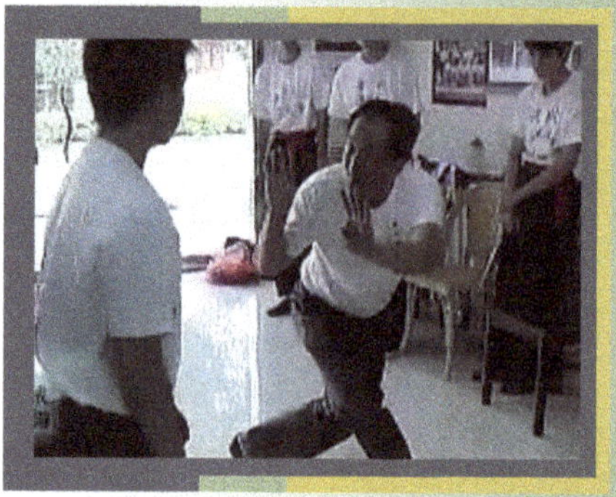

against invading marauders and many of these ancient sites still stand today as museums.

The hilly seashore topography is topped by "Seven Lady" mountain on the Dapeng Peninsula, 867 meters high. In this subtropical climate, most days are comfortable to hot with 335 days a year frost-free and an average 80% humidity. The coastal scenery of the area has been described as the most beautiful in Guangdong and even in China, with clichés such as "Hawaii in the East" and "Pearl of Shenzhen".

The area teems with fresh seafood of all kinds, as well as, fruits, such as, lychee, mango, longan and oranges. Mineral resources, such as, gold, tin, wolfram, molybdenum, copper, iron sulphide, quartzite, as well as, building materials, such as, fresh water sand, marble, granite and limestone are abundant.

The Longgang district has a population of more than one million people and there are some ten main townships; Longgang, Buji, Henggang, Kengzi, Kuichong, Dapeng, Nan'ao, Pingdi, Pinghu and Pingshan.

Pingshan—Open Area Mountain Town

Pingshan Town, just a twenty minute drive from Longgang, covers a total area of 132.8 square kilometers, and has a total population of more than three hundred thousand people. Since 2001, "the spring wind of modern culture is everywhere", in Pingshan.

This bustling Town is only 52 miles by sea to Hong Kong. As the county seat, many beautiful attractions are located in less than an hours drive away. And with major highways and roads heading in every direction, getting there is only half the fun.

It not only actively promotes the development of local and foreign business and trade, culture and education, health care, real estate, finance, and tourism with an emphasis on security, environmental standards and infrastructure, but also promotes middle and high grade hotels, recreation halls, sport activities, and cinema.

At least, once or twice a week,

starting about 8am, a mini-van comes through my neighborhood with loudspeakers announcing the local fare of the day, be it the current movie at the theater or the newest health care facility, urging you to come in for a check up.

And just down the road and up Maluan Mountain, a new international golf course is under construction. It truly is beautiful. At the summit, under the pavilion, not only can you see the expansive greens winding over the hills, but you can also see in the far distance, across the sea, Hong Kong.

Dongjiang—East River Significance

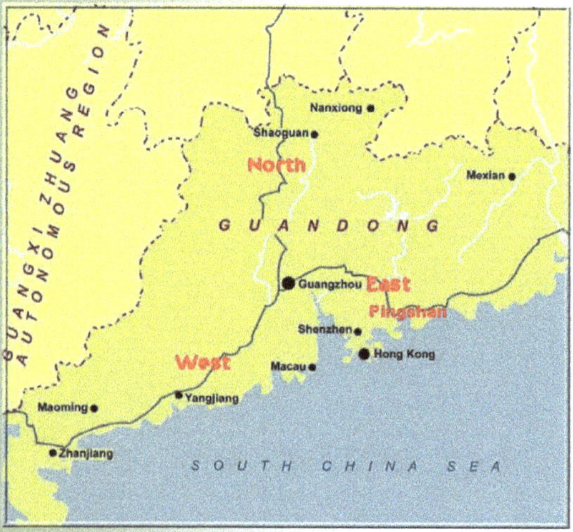

The third largest river in China is the Pearl (Zhujiang) and it flows through six provinces.

It has three tributaries in Guangdong Province; the North River (Beijiang), West River (Xijiang) and East River (Dongjiang). Be-

cause the "Dongjiang" east (Dong) river (Jiang) is literally in east Guangdong province, the appellation of 'East River' has often been applied to Som Dot's Mantis Kungfu.

However, the East River has no special significance other than giving the water of life to those in and out of the area. It is a river that does not reach the sea, but joins the Pearl River and contributes to its waters.

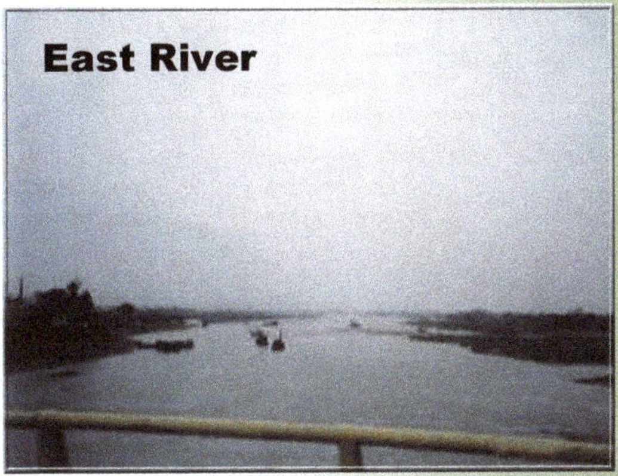

The eastern province of Jiangxi (Kwongsai) has enacted a regulation to ensure clean water supply to Hong Kong and other provinces from the headwaters of the Dongjiang River, which is the major potable water source for the region. The regulation sets responsibilities for the counties in the Dongjiang River Valleys to protect forest and water resources and stop any environmental degeneration within two years, so that Hong Kong, with a population of 7 million, can get enough quality potable water. Hong Kong island has also considered de-salination of salt water.

Since 1963, the government has invested billions in the construction of the East River-Shenzhen Water Supply Improvement Project to meet the need for water.

Although, Greenpeace reports high levels of E coli and mercury in the East River water, local governments have taken many measures to improve the ecosystem around the river and you can still explore the Pearl River Delta by super-fast ferry or air conditioned coach or train.

Spend one day or a week—from golf to sightseeing, from culinary tours to exploring temples, there is a program of discovery for everyone — Including the hometown of Kwongsai Jook Lum Temple Praying Mantis Kungfu—Pingshan Town!

To learn more about
Southern Mantis Hakka Kungfu, read the next chapter.

Mantis Boxing Principles
Warrior Intent - Willpower
Rooting
Centering
Body Posture
Ging - Explosive Force
Fist Methods
Footwork
Solo Training
Paired Training
Vital Point

Epitaph of Wong Yuk Kong

Wong Meets his Master by the East River

It was in the town of Pingshan, then truly a village, circa 1940's, that Wong Yuk Kong opened his first school.

Master Wong Yuk Kong, learned from master Chung Yel Chong. As a kungfu master, Wong was patient, with an interest to teach, hardworking, and had an unselfishness to teach all his knowledge.

Wong, as a teenager, met his master, Chung Yel Chong, beside the 'East River'. Wong was impressed by Mr. Chung's extraordinary kungfu and his good manner and so became his student.

Master Wong taught the Kwongsai Dragon Tiger Taoist Tai Chi Chuan also.

A Grandmaster is one who teaches another to become a master. There are many who still teach Wong Yuk Kong's hand today, in the USA, England, and Hong Kong, not the least of places mentioned.

In the first three years, he was taught only the basics, although, he still practiced hard every day. His master, observing his sincerity, decided to teach him all the praying mantis kungfu, internal and external, soft and hard, and the medicine.

In another four years time, he was able to understand absolutely the main points of the body posture and breathing, as well as the staff and sword.

Since, he had attained a solid foundation, any kind of change did not bother him at all. Afterwards, his teacher decided to give Mr. Wong his own school and asked him to fulfill his dream on the upper and lower streams of the East River.

He took many students and they were all treated the same, slow or fast, mind or ability.

Master Wong tried his best to help them all to become a success.

He encouraged the higher level students not to look down on the younger brothers, even though they may have more training, and taught them the higher purpose of kungfu was for health and fitness and the continuation of Chinese culture.

As a martial art teacher, Master Wong encouraged his students to exchange with other "pai" or other schools so they would be experienced in the exchange of techniques, and although, his kungfu was outstanding, he never seriously hurt anyone in order to win. Other masters and "pai" treated him like a brother-friend and he became famous because of his gentlemanly behavior.

Many people travelled from far distances to become Master Wong's students and then taught in their own areas, as he was known to be good-hearted and open-minded! Especially, in regards to his kungfu.

In fact, Master Wong never limited himself in learning. He studied and practiced other people's systems and was able to understand the advantages and disadvantages of other styles. Therefore, his teaching of praying mantis was the result of a broad understanding.

He invented the "mui fa" plum flower fist. And the "chu sa cheung" in which he would concentrate all his power in one finger to attack. All who had experienced his skill were impressed.

Grandmaster
Wong Yuk Kong
(Huang Yao Guang)
1916 - 1968

After moving to Hong Kong and opening several schools, Master Wong had truly taught more than one thousand students. His friendly and easy going personality made everyone feel happy and comfortable.

Unfortunately, nature is always jealous of the outstanding one and Master Wong died at 52 years old. Before he passed away, he asked all his students to his bedside where he repeated many times the important points of his system and medicine.

Now, the system is able to be carried on because of those who shared the spirit of master Wong, that is, "teach others all that he knew."

Hong Kong Hung Hum Praying Mantis Pai Health Fitness School 1968

Rooting in Southern Mantis
Rooting is the skill of developing the force of one thousand pounds in the feet. With it, the stance is as firm as Mt. Tai and not easily moved. Without rooting, the power of the fist will be stagnated in the chest and one's feet will not be steady allowing him to be easily thrown about.

Wong Opens the Highest Martial Hall

Wong Secretly Trains Mantis in Opium Den

The uncle of fourth generation Kwongsai Bamboo Forest Temple Mantis ancestor, Wong Yuk Kong, ran an opium den in the Ma Sai area which was frequented by Chung Yel Chong in the 1920's and 30's.

Wong Yuk Kong, as a young boy, worked in the opium den pouring tea and secretly watched Chung Yel Chong practice Southern Mantis Kungfu. After some time, Chung found the young Wong practicing Praying Mantis better than his own students and so accepted him as a disciple and taught him the three orders of Monk Som Dot as passed on by Monk Lee Siem.

After following Chung Yel Chong for some years, Wong Yuk Kong opened the first "Tong" on Ancestor Chung's behalf in the Dan Sui District of Guangdong province circa. 1940's known as the "Shang Mo Tong" or Highest Martial Hall.

1962 Hong Kong, The banner states Wong Yuk Kong's Kwongsai Bamboo Forest Temple Praying Mantis Clan.

A second was then opened on today's Changqing Street in Pingshan and was known as the "Kong Mo Tong" or Tong of "Kong's" martial art (Wong Yuk Kong). This second Tong was instructed by Wong Yuk Kong's students, Lok Wei Ping and Dai Yel Choy (refer to 1962 Hong Kong Praying Mantis Fitness Society photo in the Appendices).

A third "Kwong Mo Tong" was opened in the Longgang district and a fourth "Kwoon" or "Guan" was also opened in Huizhou.

A Tong is explained as a meeting hall or a kind of town hall in which many people come to find brother-friendship, material relief and food. Each member of Wong Yuk Kong's Tong was expected to bring a sack of rice for the common benefit of all.

A Kwoon or Guan in contrast was a school setup for the promotion of Praying Mantis and to the benefit of the Teacher's livelihood.

It is said at the time of Wong Yuk Kong's Tongs in these Hakka districts that most people participated so they might have food to eat. Those were difficult times indeed.

By the end of the 1940's, all of Wong Yuk Kong's Tongs and Guan had moved to the Huizhou district where more people lived.

There, an herbal Clinic and Kungfu school was opened and remained during the 1950's. In 1958, Wong Yuk Kong also opened the BoAi Clinic and Hospital in Pingshan.

From the early to mid 1960's, Wong Yuk Kong moved to Hong Kong as an illegal immigrant and opened five schools. Back home, his family was persecuted a bit because of his illegal status.

The first Hong Kong school was opened in Wanchai, later in Tsu-

en Wan, Yuen Long, Hong Hom and Kwon Tong. Circa. 1963, an incident occurred at the "Tien Huo Chuan Guan" Dock Workers Union in which three Sifu, asked by a number of sailors, opposed Wong Yuk Kong in an effort to gain control of the Union.

Not able to pass Wong's hand they asked a "Shen Gong" (Spirit Boxer) Sifu to place a spell upon him. It is said that Wong actually went a bit mad, climbing up walls, only to eventually have three worms come out of the top of his head, after which time, he returned to himself and continued his teaching.

The old "Shen Gong" or Spirit Shrine of Wong Yuk Kong.

It is also said, he sought the "Shen Kong" of Chung Yel Chong's mother (who was of the White Lotus Order) to counter the possession.

On July 19, 1957, Wong Yuk Kong recorded the written

history of what is simply called "Praying Mantis" today as passed down to him by Chung Yel Chong from Lee Siem Si.

It states that Som Dot was originally raised in Tibet. He was invited to Kwongsai (Jiangxi) Province Mount Dragon Tiger by Chang Tien Shih (the Taoist Pope) where he learned a Tai Chi boxing and sword as well as the Taoist herbal medicine.

It was also said that Monk Som Dot excelled at many types of Shaolin Boxing and medicine.

Author's note: I, RDH, was one year old, almost, when Wong Yuk Kong wrote down this history of Kwongsai Mantis in China. I'm fifty-five years old as of this writing. I've seen the original document and I've deliberated on the matter and come to the conclusion that since the senior and elder masters in Hong Kong and China repeat the same story, there must be truth in it.

To know how the Monk Som Dot transmitted Southern Praying Mantis, you must read the next chapter.

Contact—Control—Strike
This principle of contact, control and strike (until the opponent is red) is central to all mantis action and is based on the three powers of the arm; from the shoulder to the elbow, elbow to the wrist, wrist to the fingertips.

Written History of Southern Praying Mantis in China

Monk Som Dot Transmits Three Orders of Mantis

It is said that after arriving on Dragon Tiger Mountain, Som Dot accepted two disciples, Wong Leng, an illiterate, but diligent disciple, and Lee Siem.

Lee Siem later became known as Siem Yuen, which means capable of grasping the depth of Buddhism. And Wong Leng became known as Wong Do (Tao) Yuen, capable of grasping Taoism.

After some years, Som Dot sent his two disciples down the mountain to spread his art of Shaolin, which was divided into three orders.

Monk Som Dot Image

The first and highest order teaches the principle of 10 soft and one hard, and was taught only on the top of the mountain.

The second order is half hard, half soft. The third order is based on extremely forceful technique. This is the reason the art is sometimes called a "three door or gate" art today.

In doing so, as they descended the mountain, Wong Do Yuen and Lee Siem Yuen, at the middle gate of the mountain accepted a student named Chu Long Bot. Hiding the kungfu of the first order, they taught Chu Long Bot only the second order kungfu of Som Dot. At that time, the first order kungfu of Som Dot was not taught.

After learning the art, Chu, having no knowledge of the first order kungfu, betrayed Wong and Lee and used only the Chu name to pass on what was called Chu Gar Gao or Chu's Creed.

Chu Long Bot later taught Chu An Nam, who taught Yang Sao and Lao Sui, who was a friend of Chu Kwei, who was the father of Chu Kwong Hua in contemporary times (refer to the 1962

Hong Kong Praying Mantis Fitness Society photograph). This order of kungfu was originally taught only at the middle gate of the mountain.

Monk Lee Siem Image

Later, as Wong Do Yuen and Lee Siem Yuen went back down the mountain, at the lower gate, a praying mantis insect popped out in front of them. Wong, being the first to step off the mountain, proclaimed the mantis must be a sign from Heaven and to avoid further persecution of Som Dot's Shaolin teaching, the Shaolin art of three orders should be called Praying Mantis.

At the bottom of the mountain, a man named, Choy Tit Ngau, (Ngau / Niu means Ox) pleaded with sincerity to learn their kungfu and the two of them taught him Som Dot's third order of kungfu based on extremely forceful techniques.

Not knowing what to call the art, Choy, having no knowledge of the first or second order of Som Dot, eventually did the same as the Chu Clan and called the art Tit Ngau, or Iron Ox. Later Chung Lo Ku learned from Choy and passed on this teaching as Chung Gar Gao in the East River region. This kungfu of the

Wong Yuk Kong plays the broadswords, 1962.

third order was taught at the bottom of the mountain. (Refer to the Iron Ox interview).

Authors note: The story of Chu Long Bot and Wong Do Yuen is one that I first heard from Sifu Louie Jack Man. I became Louie Sifu's mantis student circa. 1977, in Kentucky. Mark Gin Foon Sifu, circa. 1980, also repeated the story of a three door system in Minnesota. —RDH

As no one had yet used the "Tanglang" name to pass on Som Dot's teaching, Lee Siem went back down the mountain to find someone to learn and carry on the name. He accepted two students, Xie Yun Fei and Chung Yel Chung . It is said that Xie learned the art of "chinggong" light body skill and was exceptional at climbing trees and over houses. Xie was sent by Lee Siem to the northern five provinces to spread Som Dot's kungfu. And Chung was sent to the southern seven provinces. (Can you name them?)

Wong Yuk Kong died in 1968 at the age of 52. The cause of death has never been determined. However, soon afterwards, Yip Sui, who changed the name of Chu Long Bot's Chu Gar to

Chow Gar, disclosed information to the press that erroneously stated Wong Yuk Kong stole Tanglang from Chu Kwong Hua. At the time, six of Wong Yuk Kong's students collected the prodigious amount of $60,000 Hong Kong dollars and put it aside for bail, before challenging Yip Sui and Chu Gar.

Wong Yuk Kong plays the broadswords, 1962.

As a result, Yip Sui is said to have closed his school and gone incognito. At first, Chu Kwong Hua, as head of Chu Gar and Lao Sui's successor, was displeased with Yip Sui and apologized to the elder son of Wong Yuk Kong. Later, Yip Sui, is said to have also apologized. (See the Appendices—Reliquary Photos of Wong Yuk Kong and Yip Sui in Wong's Association).

Author's note: I first heard this, in the USA, circa 1989, from my Chu Gar teacher, Chen Ching Hong (Eugene Chen). It has been restated several times since, by many different Sifu, giving it credence. I have fond memories of Yip Sui. I often was the emissary between him and his also, late disciple, Choy Kam Man. I still have his photographs, letters and videos that will remain personal. I published magazine articles for both Yip Sui and Choy Kam Man. —RDH

One Hand Controls Two
A skillful mantis will defend and attack using one arm to trap and control the opponents two arms, leaving one hand to attack freely at will.

Four Wong Brothers - Inheritors of Kwongsai Mantis

Wong's Sons Receive and Transmit the Art

Wong Yuk Kong, in his 52 years, had two wives, four sons and one daughter. Although all of them have been actively involved in one fashion or another in receiving and transmitting the Kwongsai Bamboo Temple Art and Wong's heritage, it can be said that two have specialized in carrying forward and one, Wong Yu Hua, is actively teaching Southern Praying Mantis and the Hakka Unicorn culture in the hometown of Pingshan today.

It is untrue, as some have stated, that Wong did not transmit Southern Praying Mantis to his family or leave a heritage. There stories may read like fiction to some, but where there is smoke there is fire.

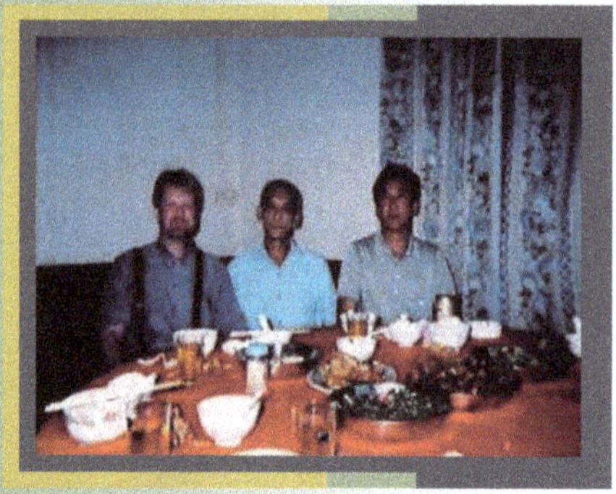

Wong Yao Fei, Second Son

Ancestor Wong Yuk Kong's second eldest son with Southern Mantis Kungfu, Wong Yao Fei, 63 (2012), left photo center, has suffered many personal hardships.

It is recorded that in one incident, in Hong Kong, where he lives, he had defeated some score of people in an altercation, only to be finally thrown from a high rise building and survive. Inspired by Shen Kong (Spirit Possession), he simply got up and walked away as witnessed. The story was carried in the Hong Kong newspapers. Today he is weathered in appearance and terse in words.

Photo left: RDH left; Wong Yao Hua, fourth son, right. Photo right: Wong Family Meals in Hakka Restaurants always courtesy of Wong Yu Hua. Special thanks to Annie Zhong.

Author's note: The story of Yao Fei's descent was repeated to me in several different versions by several different people and is more bizarre than I have written here. However, as stated before, where there is smoke there is fire. There must be some truth in it.

I have never met the eldest son of Wong Yuk Kong, Wong Yu Ming, although, I have made the acquaintance of his daughter, Wong Bi Yuen. ---RDH

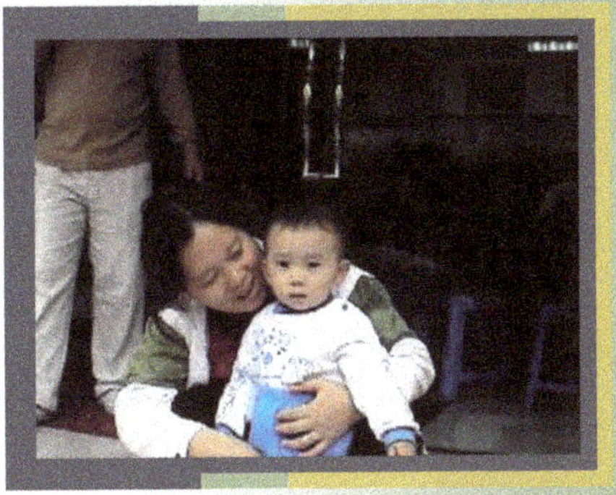

Wong Yao Hong, Third Son

Although, at first, being denied by his father to learn Tanglang because he was a naughty boy, Yu Hua is said to have eventually received 90% of his father, Wong Yuk Kong's, teaching.

In the 1970's, he travelled to Spain where he demonstrated "mui-fa" plum flower pole which was popularly hailed. At that time, due to his popularity, he was challenged by and bested three southern style practitioners.

He has also travelled to Toronto, Canada and London, England to promote Tanglang. Today, he has one student in Australia who operates a Tong. And although, he doesn't teach openly, it is obvious that he is "Tanglang".

Photo upper left: Wong Yao Hong. Upper Right: Yao Hong's young son—grandson of Yuk Kong. Middle: Wong Yao Hong as a youngster. Lower: Yao Hong as a young boy plays Som Gin.

Wong Yuk Kong's family and children obviously received the Bamboo Temple Art transmission and his family heritage. As fourth son says, "I am not one to speak ill. These are the iron facts and should not be changed or distorted to suit one's personal interest. —Wong Yao Hua

Wong Yao Hong, above, is 61 (2012). It's easy to see the enthusiasm on his face for Southern Mantis even as a young man.

Author's note: I am well acquainted with Wong Yao Hong and we are friends. He has and expresses a great deal of martial intent in his practice and performances. He does not hesitate to show or cross his hands. You can view the video demonstrations in the China Southern Mantis Survey eBook: www.chinamantis.com.

L) Wong Yu Hua Sifu is respected in Hong Kong and South China

Wong Yao Hua, Fourth Son

Although, never having trained with his father, Wong Yu Hua, 53, (2012) had the good fortune to learn directly from his elder uncles and brothers.

Among those are uncles (refer to this Survey interviews) Yao Kam Fat, Xu Fat Chun, Yang Gun Ming, and older Brother Lai Wei Keung, not to mention Chung Yel Chong's student, Chen Poon, (passed in 1980's), who was also a friend of Chu Gar Gao teacher, Lao Sui.

Yao Hua stresses Brother-friendship today and that there is no best kungfu, no number one. And that kungfu should never be used for undesirable purposes.

Upon meeting several of Brother Yao Hua's teacher's and their relatives it was said of him by, Yao Kam Fat, 80, "Yao Hua was a naughty boy with exceptional skill who I couldn't do a thing with."

Xu Fat Chun, Iron Ox Pai and student of Wong Yuk Kong as well, was quoted as saying, "You are your father's son", and Yang Gun Ming was quoted as saying, "I am satisfied that Yu Hua is Wong Yuk Kong's son who will carry forward his skill and art."

Guang Wu Tang, China Intangible Cultural Heritage Award 2009

From the age of 13, Yu (Yao) Hua, practiced the Dit Da medicine and the Tanglang kungfu. He was recognized in a local martial art competition as one who competed and excelled in five different events in one competition.

In 1984, Wong Yao Hua, opened his first school in Pingshan named after his son, Wong Xing Jong.

He is quoted as saying, "Iron steps are firm but flexible, hear the opponents sound, see his shadow, move accordingly; From the feet, waist, and shoulders power will arrive in the hands. Float, sink, swallow and spit principles are from three points; feet, waist and shoulders as one."

The original Kwongsai Tanglang still exists in Pingshan Town today. According to Yu Hua, those of his father's students who learned in the 1930 and 40's are different than those who learned after the 1960's, when his father, Wong Yuk Kong, added more soft power to the Tanglang practice. He further stated, in the early Tong (meeting hall), seniority was by age and not by time spent in the school.

There were hundreds of people and many different kungfu groups and teachers celebrating this day. The only clash I saw

Wong Sifu (center in blue)
Ma Sai (Chung Yel Chong Family)

Author, RDH & Wong Yu Hua
Pingshan Guang Wu Tang

was two unicorns didn't seem to recognize each other. There were no lions dancers that day. Likely, because this was almost solely a Hakka Celebration, and the Unicorn is a Hakka symbol.

When a lion (earth) and a Unicorn (Heaven) meet, it is customary for the lion to bow to the Unicorn. If not, a clash may erupt with one attempting to dislodge and knock the others head to the ground.

With a wave of Wong Sifu's hand, the Unicorn conflict was over and the ceremonies continued as both Unicorns and their Sifu payed respect at the Ancestral Shrine. ---RDH

To know more details of
Monk Som Dot's transmission, read the next chapter.

China Jook Lum Temple Boxing

Wong Yuk Kong circa 1960:

Dan Jong: Single Arm Form
Shuang Jong: Two Arms Form
Three Scissors Shaking Bridge
Four Doors Fist Form
Flexible Fists and Feet Form
Refining the Bridge Form
Strike a Sandbag Form
Uncommon Form Method
Eight Doors Fighting Form
Plum Flower Form

China's Southern Mantis History Reiterated

Monk Som Dot's Transmission Further Elucidated

It was a pleasure to see many groups and Sifu all in accord at the 35th Anniversary Celebration for the late Wong Yuk Kong Sifu. There are many young mantids today that will bring the China transmission of the Art along.

The Standard (banner or flag) shown says, Kwongsai Bamboo Forest Temple Praying Mantis Clan; Martial Virtue is the Sifu's Way; The Pen and the Sword.

As hundreds of people milled about before the celebration be-

35th Anniversary Celebration of Wong Yuk Kong's Kwongsai Mantis

gan, upfront Unicorns and Sifus alike paid respect at the Ancestral Shrine, while out back, folks gathered to watch various Hakka Southern Mantis programs, including the Wong Fei Hong versus Jook Lum Temple movie on TV, in anticipation of the evening meal including lobsters, shrimps, fish, beef, pork, chicken and an assortment of local vegetables and Hakka dishes. (Refer to www.mantisflix.com for the movie.)

The red banner over the TV states, "35th Anniversary of Wong Yuk Kong's passing; Kwongsai Jook Lum Temple Praying Mantis National Art.

Sifu Lee Chun Lim at the Ancestral Shrine

Some time past, I travelled with Wong Yu Hua and his family when they were buying their first son a home. The home was in a high rise and the view was beautiful looking over Shenzhen.

At that time, Wong Yu Hua further elucidated his father's written history of Tanglang saying, "Lee Siem Si and Wong Do Yuen went down the mountain and travelled about as doctors curing patients. They accepted two disciples; Chu Long Bot and Chu An Nam.

35th Anniversary Celebration of Wong Yuk Kong's Kwongsai Mantis

Wong Do Yuen taught Som Dot's kungfu classified in three orders; the first order was named Chiang Fung, Upper Order; Yi Fung, Second Order, and Som Fung, Third Order.

Wong Do Yuen taught Chu Long Bot and Chu An Nam, the second order kungfu. At that time the upper order kungfu was never taught to others.

It was Chu An Nam who changed the name of Som Dot's kungfu to Chu Gar Gao, not knowing what else to call it. He taught Lao Sui and Chu Kwei who was the father of Chu Kwong Hua, teacher of Cheng Wan (2005, aged 81).

After a period, Lee Siem Yuen and Wong Do Yuen went down to Hong Kong and Macau and found that Som Dot's Tanglang boxing was being called Chu Gar Gao, so they felt unhappy.

When the Mountain was burned by Authorities, during the escape of the burning, the two of them met Choy Tit Ngau, who recognized their kungfu was very useful, so he invited Lee Siem to be his teacher many times.

Author's note: Sifu Lai Wei Keung, whose troupe provided the Hakka music, is not shy about his understanding. He was the first instructor allowed to teach by Wong Yuk Kong, in the Shang Mo Tong, circa. 1940's, Pingshan Town.

35th Anniversary Celebration of Wong Yuk Kong's Kwongsai Mantis

At 83 or so now (2012), he is often one the first to stand up for mantis. See what he says was only taught in those early days in the Volume 2 Book, China Mantis Reunion—RDH (China Southern Mantis Survey eBook www.chinamantis.com)

Wong and Lee discussed it over time, and according to the figure and strength of Choy Tit Ngau, decided to teach him the third order of kungfu based on hard strength, which includes two sets of boxing; Yi Mun (Two Gate) and Som Mun (Three Gate). Choy Tit Ngau's art was passed on to Chung Lo Ku who later named it Chung Gar Gao. Chung Gar Gao, from Iron Ox, still exists today in the Hakka areas of the East River.

Lee Siem and Wong Do Yuen went down to Hong Kong and on the way met Chung Yel Chong, whose mother was an acrobat. She knew of Lee and Wong and told them that Tanglang had changed the name to Chu Gar Gao in Hong Kong and the Pearl Delta (East River) valley.

Later Lee, Wong and the young Chung Yel Chong went to Wu Tai Shan - Five Peaks Mountain. On the way, they met an acrobat from North China whose kungfu was good. He was Xie Yun Fei and was three years older than Chung Yel Chung. Then, they all four went up Wu Tai Shan to the Jook Lum Temple. There, Lee and Wong taught the two, Chung and Xie, Som Dot's upper order

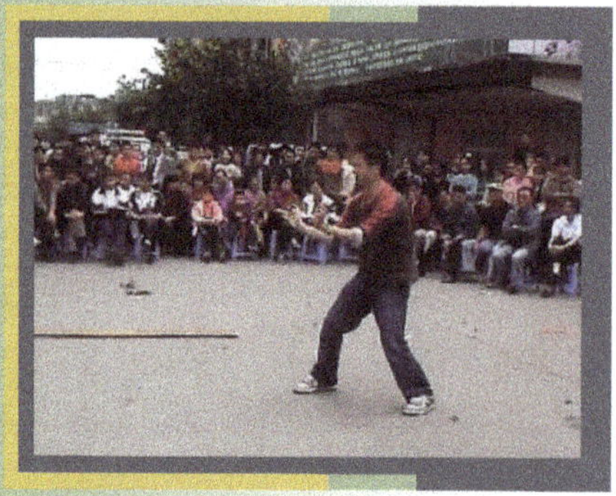

35th Anniversary Celebration of Wong Yuk Kong's Kwongsai Mantis

kungfu of 10 soft one hard.

Chung and Xie mastered Som Dot's upper order kungfu and went down the mountain and parted. Xie went to the north and Chung went down to the seven Southern Provinces (Henan, Hubei, Hunan, Guangxi, Jiangxi (Kwongsai), Guangdong, Hainan).

After Chung Yel Chong went south, he found Lao Sui, who was calling the art, Chu Gar Gao. Chung wanted to correct the name to Tanglang boxing and so Lao Sui and Chung closed the door and exchanged kungfu together and discovered their kungfu was from the same root and family. Afterwards, Lao Sui agreed to call it, Chu Gar Tanglang, which represented the two orders, second (Chu) and upper (Tanglang).

Author's note: Today, in Hong Kong, Chu Gar is referred to as Chu Gar Tanglang. In another anecdote, I've been asked not to reveal, Chung went to the hometown of Chu Gar Gao (Mei County) and exchanged skill.

On another note, although, I appreciate the cultural importance of Unicorn dancing, I must admit always being a bit 'bored' by the number of demonstrations. However, "Tanglang without Unicorns is like Tanglang without Lee Siem's Dit Da Jow Formula ...it is not Tanglang," as others have said.

35th Anniversary Celebration of Wong Yuk Kong's Kwongsai Mantis

Look to the addendums for the Dit Da formula. It contains some 47 ingredients, most which can only be hand picked on the mountains of the area, and is based in vinegar not wine. It takes one night under a special moon to prepare. I have accompanied Yu Hua in the overnight preparation and often use the "bruise medicine." There are some six or eight barrels brewing at the back of his home which come out at 32 degrees, by volume. Bruises quickly disappear, but you are sometimes left with a skin rash. ---RDH

According to the records of Wong Yuk Kong, Chung Yel Chong said, "Tanglang kungfu was classified into three types; Chiang Fung, 10 soft, one hard; Yi Fung, half hard-half soft; and Som Fung, hard strength and hard horse. And each order had its advantage and each is worthwhile to learn and study.

In the 30's to 40's Chung Yel Chung took Wong Yuk Kong around Hui Yang and Hong Kong and taught Tanglang kungfu and medicine. Chung and Wong helped the Dongguan guerillas to cure injured patients freely.

It is said, Master Chung was killed by a Japanese bomb in Shaoguan, Guangdong. In memory of Chung, Wong set up four large Tongs in the Huiyang District; Dan Sui Tong was Kong Mo Tong, Pingshan was Kong Mo Tong, Liangjiang was Yin Mo

35th Anniversary Celebration of Wong Yuk Kong's Kwongsai Mantis

Tong, and Longgang was the Shang Mo Tong.

Author's note: The Pingshan mantis youth demonstrations remind me of Mark Gin Foon Sifu's "Loose Hands" and the opening and closing of most of his weapons sets in the late 1970's and early 80's. ---RDH

During the end of the 50's, Wong Yuk Kong widely taught kungfu in the Huiyang area. In 1958, the Chinese Herbal United Clinic was founded.

Especially, from 1959-61, Wong taught government officials Chang Tien Shih's, Dragon Tiger Mountain, Tai Chi boxing and sword sets to build up their bodies. In 1962, Wong went to Hong Kong again and established five schools in various districts and taught Tanglang without reservation.

Author's note: Some postures strongly resemble a posture in the "three steps forward" set that Sifu Sammy Wong taught in the Chicago area and demonstrated on local Chicago TV. These youth demonstrations are students of Sifu Lai Wei Keung ---RDH

Wong Yu Hua Sifu ended this reiteration by saying, "Before we end this talk today, I appeal to all Tanglang disciples to love and respect the history and blossom the art. These are the iron facts

35th Anniversary Celebration of Wong Yuk Kong's Kwongsai Mantis

about Tanglang and shouldn't be changed or made up to suit one's self or purpose".

Author's note: During the time we were at Yu Hua's son's new home, of course, we looked over the various rooms and discussed what should go where, but it took a few hours, just to write this addendum to Tanglang history down. Afterwards, we simply drove back to Pingshan, that day a little more than one hour's drive. ---RDH

To know what followed, read on.

Southern Mantis Posture

Practitioners emulate the mantis fighting posture by extending their hands forward, with the elbows slightly bent and tucked in close to protect the centerline - like a mantis. The feet are separated by the distance of about 18-24 inches, shoulder width apart, with the bent lead leg supporting most of the weight, while the slightly curved leg acts as a strut.

Master Chung Blossoms Hakka Mantis in South China

Master Chung Yel Chong Brings Mantis To South China

One leisurely discussion of the Pingshan Mantis Celebration centered around the history of Chung Yel Chong, third Ancestor of Kwongsai Jook Lum Temple Mantis, and his journey with Monk Lee Siem to the Jook Lum Temple at Wu Tai Shan Five Peaks Mountain in Northern Shanxi Province.

Chung Yel Chong accompanied Monk Lee Siem to the Wu Tai Shan Bamboo Temple in order to practice Kungfu and study medicine. Ultimately, Chung mastered these pursuits and in

35th Anniversary Celebration of Wong Yuk Kong's Kwongsai Mantis

1917, Master Chung and his teacher left Wu Tai Shan and travelled back to south China. It is said, the journey took them six months by horseback to return to the South.

During the 1920's Master Chung opened a number of Schools in Hong Kong and South China. Refer to the Volume 4 Book of the Survey for complete details and an Interview with Chung's family.

Chung's Kwongsai Mantis teaching was based on actual combat applications with techniques such as hidden force, phoenix eye fists, club hand, and nail knees with power from the Dan Tien (navel). Having earned the nickname, "King of the Staff", he incorporated the "34 Points Plum Blossom Staff " to commemorate his teacher.

In 1917, Master Chung and Lee Siem left the Jook Lum Temple in Shanxi by horseback. The journey took them six months to return to South China! For more about Master Chung refer to the Volume 4 Book, On Som Dot's Trail.

After returning to Pingshan, Chung opened a school in the Ma Sai area which housed the Lam (Lam Sang's family) Clan on one side of the road and the Chung Clan on the other.

35th Anniversary Celebration of Wong Yuk Kong's Kwongsai Mantis

Today, 2012, in the Pingshan Town, Ma Sai area, the descendants of Chung Yel Chong still operate a Unicorn and Kwongsai Mantis Hall under the same name as the Wong Yuk Kong family—the Guang Wu Tang.

Some say, during the war at Liaozhou, Chung Yel Chong disappeared and no one knows if he lived or died. He was and remains a mysterious figure.

Today, 2012, in the Pingshan Town, Ma Sai area, the descendants of Chung Yel Chong still operate a Unicorn and Kwongsai Mantis Hall under the same name as the Wong Yuk Kong family—the Guang Wu Tang.

It is said that the two people who obtained the secrets of the style from Chung Yel Chong were Wong Yuk Kong and Lam Sang. After Master Lam Sang had left Hong Kong for the UK in the 1940's, it was Wong Yuk Kong who had cared for the family of their master, Chung Yel Chong.

Many relatives of Chung Yel Chong, as well as, elder Mantis players remain in the Dan Sui district today. The Hakka are a large minority. At the time of this writing, the Chung family

35th Anniversary Celebration of Wong Yuk Kong's Kwongsai Mantis

lives very comfortably within a large gated area, three generations under one roof, including both grandsons and their families and their mother. None of Chung's immediate family admit to practice Mantis today, only the Kwongsai Jook Lum Temple Dit Da Medicine.

However, the extended (Zhang) Chung Yel Chong Clan in Ma Sai, Pingshan Town has published of late the following letter publicly:

江西竹林寺螳螂派「馬岭國術會 悅來堂」的歷史簡介

Brief History of the Mantis Sect of Yuelai House of Maling Martial Art Society, Zhulin Temple, Jiangxi Province (Jook Lum Temple, Kwongsai Province)

本人張忠誠(阿鏡)，據我阿公張戊申(鋼伯)及長輩的憶述，江西竹林寺螳螂派功夫的源頭，始祖三達祖師(西藏人)身懷螳螂派功夫的絕技及精湛醫術，雲遊四海至山西五台山竹林寺後到江西龍虎山修煉禪法，傳授武學及醫術，傳下門徒有黃道人和李禪師，這樣江西竹林寺螳螂派功夫在中原流傳開去。

I'm Zhang Zhongcheng (Ah Jing), per recall of my grandpa Zhang Wushen (Gang Bo) and the other seniors, the origin of Jiangxi Zhulin Temple Mantis Sect is the Ancestor, Master Sanda (Som Dot) a Tibetan.

35th Anniversary Celebration of Wong Yuk Kong's Kwongsai Mantis

He was highly skillful in the Mantis kungfu and medicine. He traveled widely in the world and came to Longhu (Dragon-Tiger) Mountain for practice after visiting Wutai Mountain's Zhulin Temple in Shanxi. He taught kungfu and medicine there and his students included Taoist Priest Huang (Wong Leng) and Chan Master Li (Lee Siem). Hence, the kungfu of Jiangxi Zhulin Temple Mantis Sect later became popular in China.

師公張耀宗有緣拜李禪師學習螳螂派功夫及精湛醫術。從硬功夫開始入門練習至軟功夫，終於練成九柔一剛的功夫。1917年,師公張耀宗師承下山。後期在香港,我阿公(剛伯)之父親張雪翹巧遇師公張耀宗,二人惺惺相惜,並力邀張耀宗到當時屬惠陽縣管轄的坪山馬岭西村傳授本村張姓青少年螳螂派功夫,將螳螂派功夫發揚光大。從這刻就展開他對螳螂派事業的光輝旅程。

Our Zhang Clan —(Chung family) teacher, Master Zhang Yaozong (Chung Yel Chong) fortunately became Chan Master Li's student for learning the Mantis kungfu and fine medicine skill. He started from hard kungfu to soft kungfu and finally achieved the nine soft—one-hard kungfu. In 1917, Zhang Yaozong completed his course and left the mountain. Later in Hong Kong, Zhang Xueqiao, the father of my grandpa (Gang Bo), encountered Zhang Yaozong, and they persuaded Zhang to teach Zhang Family's young men in Malingxi Village governed by Huiyang

35th Anniversary Celebration of Wong Yuk Kong's Kwongsai Mantis

(Wai Yearn) County at that time so as to popularize the Mantis Sect kungfu. Zhang Yao Zhong (Chung Yel Chong) started the glorious journey of developing the Mantis Sect from that time.

「馬岭西村 悅來堂」全村人皆姓張。師公張耀宗當時門徒包括:我阿公張戊申（剛伯）、張九、張平、張勝、張亞基、張譚安、張就金、張牛仔、張觀昇、張進發、黃毓光......等人,人數不能盡錄。當時村內裡的長輩及師公經磋商,均同意。只傳本村張姓人。他們每天都集合在祠堂門口的空曠地鍛鍊。入夜後就點起柴火繼續操練。

Malingxi Village-Yuelai House – the entire village is of the Zhang (Chung) family name. Master's Master Zhang Yaozong's (Chung Yel Chong's) students included: my grandpa Zhang Wushen (Gang Bo), Zhang Jiu, Zhang Ping, Zhang Sheng, Zhang Yaji, Zhang Tan'an, Zhang Jiujin, Zhang Niuzai, Zhang Guansheng, Zhang Jinfa, Huang Yuguang (Wong Yuk Kong)... and other people who aren't fully listed. At that time, via negotiation and consent, only the Zhang's will be taught. They daily gathered and practiced in a court in front of the ancestral hall at daytime and continued to practice at nighttime by burning wood.

三十年代初,有一香港船公司邀請師公張耀宗到香港「天和船館」設館授徒。同行跟隨包括: 我阿公張戊申（剛伯）、張亞基、

35th Anniversary Celebration of Wong Yuk Kong's Kwongsai Mantis

張譚安、張進發、張牛仔及黃毓光……等人。這樣地,江西竹林寺螳螂派功夫就在香港落地生根了。

Early 1930's, a Hong Kong ship company invited Zhang Zongyao to set up a school in Tianhe Ship House in Hong Kong and teach students there. Those who followed him included my grandpa Zhang Wushen (Gang Bo), Zhang Yaji, Zhang Tan'an, Zhang Jinfa, Zhang Niuzai and Huang Yuguang… and others. Therefore, Jiangxi Zhulin Temple Mantis Sect's kungfu was settled in Hong Kong.

後期,我阿公張戊申（剛伯）在香港回到本村延續師公張耀宗流傳下來的螳螂派功夫及精湛醫術,將這燦爛文化及光輝成就繼續發揚光大。為了紀念三達祖師,在師公祖台上寫著「三達門中真妙手,竹林寺內煉精功」一幅對聯,代代相傳。鍛練方式，馬步不丁不八，含胸拔背，坐搏沉睜，吞吐浮沉，驚、彈、勁、搓、擒、挪、抓、捉八字真言，將江西竹林寺螳螂派功夫世世代代延續下去。

Later, my grandpa Zhang Wushen (Gang Bo) returned to our village from Hong Kong to carry on the excellent Mantis kungfu and medicine taught by Zhang Yaozong and gave cause for this great glorious culture and achievement to be inherited and developed. In order to commemorate Ancestor Master Sanda (Som Dot), an antithetical couplet is written on the worship platform of Zhang Yaozong (Chung Yel Chong) – Real Boxing Lies In Sanda (Som

35th Anniversary Celebration of Wong Yuk Kong's Kwongsai Mantis

Dot) Sect, True Kung Fu Is Formed In Zhulin Temple. It's been inherited for generations. The practicing method is this. The horse stance is neither of the shape of the Chinese character Ding or Ba. Breathe in to hold the chest and lift the back. Have a calm vision and rest to standby for battle. The 8 styles are summarized with 8 Chinese characters which mean shock, flexibility, strength, twist, capture, shift, grasp and seizure. Jiangxi Zhulin Temple Mantis Sect's kungfu is so inherited from generation to generation.

每當政府及民間的慶祝活動都會誠邀馬岭西村麒麟作慶祝表演。1988年，東江縱隊曾生司令帶領二千多名老戰士回故鄉坪山。本村麒麟就擔當了一個重要的角色，擘舞麒麟，生動傳神，令客人歡呼讚許，好評如潮。

Governments and public bodies often invited Malingxi Village Kylin Unicorn for performance in ceremonies. In 1988, Zeng Sheng, Commander of East River Column, let more than 2,000 old soldiers returned to the hometown of Pingshan. Our village's kylin Unicorn played an important role at the welcoming ceremony, winning great reputation from the public.

· 我阿公張(公)戊申(剛伯)自2002年仙遊後，在村長的積極帶領下並得到長輩及各師兄弟的鼎力支持，馬岭西村的武術心得及麒麟哲學以然繁業昌盛。在2009年的一年間，得到香港各武術界友好及同門邀請進出香港無數次作武術交流及觀摩表演。馬岭國術

35th Anniversary Celebration of Wong Yuk Kong's Kwongsai Mantis

會在過去所做的一切，得到社會認同及讚許。

After my grandpa Zhang Wushen (Gang Bo) died in 2002, under the village chief's leadership and the support of all the senior and the fellow apprentices of the same master, Malingxi Village's kungfu idea and kylin Unicorn's philosophy was then made prosperous. During 2009, for many times, we were invited by Hong Kong's kungfu friends and presented our performance in Hong Kong for culture exchange. What Maling Martial Art Society has done has won a positive comment and reputation from the kungfu community at large.

2009年本村在香港及海外註冊成立「馬嶺國術會 悅來堂」，本村的螳螂派功夫及麒麟自師公張耀宗流傳至今，要將江西竹林寺螳螂派功夫和麒麟歷史及傳統文化繼續承傳下去，有賴大家的努力及鼎力支持。本人才疏學淺，只能據我阿公及長輩的憶述，簡略道出江西竹林寺螳螂派在馬岭西村的簡短歷史，如有不足之處，敬請原諒，多多包涵。

In 2009, our village registered Maling Martial Art Society—Yuelai House in Hong Kong. The Mantis Sect kungfu and kylin Unicorn philosophy had been inherited from the time of our Master's Master, Zhang Yaozong (Chung Yel Chong). We will continue to popularize and transmit the Jiangxi Zhulin Temple Mantis Sect's

35th Anniversary Celebration of Wong Yuk Kong's Kwongsai Mantis

kungfu and kylin Unicorn history as well as the culture. Thanks to everyone's great effort and support we are able to do so. I have limited knowledge so this brief history of Jiangxi Zhulin Temple Mantis Sect in Malingxi Village, Pingshan Town is made per the recall of my grandpa, Zhang WuShen, and the other seniors. If there's something or someone missing, kindly understand it with tolerance.

Malingxi Village, Pingshan District, Shenzhen City, China
Maling Martial Art Society, Yue Lai House
Vice Chairman: Zhong Zhongcheng (Ah Jing)
Malingxi Village Council

To learn more of Hakka Mantis and culture,
read the next chapter.

Tactical Operations

A single movement of the arm may contain several actions. Tactical operations of the hand include grappling, catching, holding, capturing, clasping with the forearms, slicing strikes with the knuckles, pressing with the elbow, sudden quick pushes with both hands, spearing with extended fingers, flicking of the hands in quick jabs, exploding fingers from the fists, jerking the opponent's arm, slicing and chopping with the edge of the palm, hooking and deflecting hands, elbow strikes, claw-like raking actions, and poking with the back of the hands. Many of the movements are simultaneously defensive and offensive. The feet, ankles, knees and hips may mirror the hand movements.

Hakka Culture Along the East River

Rooted Horse, One Arm–Three Hands, Explosive Force

Within minutes from Pingshan, the Hakka's Customs Museum, is the largest dwelling house for Hakka people in China. The architecture is grand and brilliant.

Built by a Hakka, named Luo, it was completed in 1817, after several decades and three generations of continual building. It covers some 25,000 square meters and has 179 apartments for

35th Anniversary Celebration of Wong Yuk Kong's Kwongsai Mantis

dwelling, each apartment comprising several rooms.

Hakka dwellings usually have a large outside gated wall that surrounds everything inside. The outside wall is wide in the front and narrow in the back, taking the form of a silver ingot.

The inside building has high walls that separate living rooms, wells, verandas and courtyards in a labyrinth form.

Easy to defend and difficult to attack, Hakka dwellings are described as "nine layers of sky and eighteen walls, ten pavilions passing through winding verandas for horses". The Hakka's Customs Museum offers a grand view of the patriarchal clan system and kinship spirit and is of great historic value.

The Grand Forever House, southwest of Pingshan Town, is another excellent example of Hakka influence in the area. Resembling a castle, it was built in the Qing Dynasty (in the 1800's), and covers a rectangular plan of fifteen thousand square meters.

On the four corners of the rectangle, are block houses. High walls surround the outside perimeter with a large center gate that con-

35th Anniversary Celebration of Wong Yuk Kong's Kwongsai Mantis

nects the rectangle by horse passage-ways. The gate opens to the south and is inscribed, "Grand Forever House". It has garden lawns, a pond in the shape of the moon that resembles a moat, flag stands, and tortoise motifs.

The Hakka people are an ethnic group of the eight series of Han Chinese. They have distinctive individuality and are distributed widely throughout the world. Some scholars say the Hakka language is the origin of Chinese language.

The Hakka people originated from China's central plains. From the Western Jin Dynasty to the Ming and Qing Dynasty, in more than one thousand years, they moved in a large-scale five times.

Due to famine and wars, in later times, they began to migrate to Jiangxi (Kwongsai), Fujian and Guangdong. Gradually, they spread to all provinces in the south and overseas.

A large settlement developed in Meizhou, east Guangdong, Province. After that, settlements moved to the coastal areas such as Shenzhen and Hong Kong.

35th Anniversary Celebration of Wong Yuk Kong's Kwongsai Mantis

The Hakka people represent about 60% of the native residents in the Shenzhen, Longgang area. They have their own language, culture, customs, and house patterns and are distinctly Hakka.

Heyuan, Northeastern Guangdong Province, is a tourist city with picturesque sceneries, delicious foods, as well as, colorful Hakka culture and customs. The Town's first Hakka Culture Tourism Festival was held earlier this year (2004).

A lion dance team, named "Golden Lion," with 60 dancers and six "Golden Lions", took part in a series of folk art performances during the festival.

No one, Hakka, here, refers to mantis, or any of their many styles of martial art, as Hakka. Neither do they distinct "south mantis". In fact, Hakka people here, in China, strongly oppose saying, "southern praying mantis." They simply refer to Kwongsai Mantis, Chugar Mantis or Iron Ox. But, it is true that many of their martial arts often look the same. And, every Hakka clan seems to have their own family art.

35th Anniversary Celebration of Wong Yuk Kong's Kwongsai Mantis

However, there does seem to be a commonality to all of them; the stance is short, the arm always seems to have three hands, and there is "ging", explosive force.

Cultural Anecdote

Hakka women, today, still have a habit of wearing 'cooling hats', which are woven with thin bamboo strips, in a circle, with a hole as big as human's head, in the center.

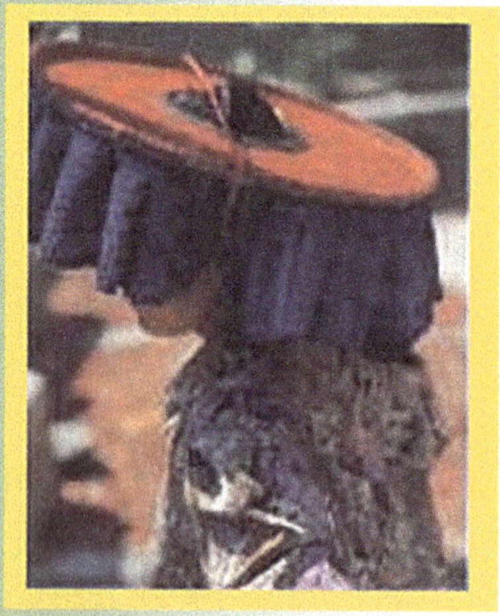

This hat generally has a diameter of about 50 cm, with blue strips suspended on its edges.

From the view of history, a woman should stay in her house all day, but, in order to make a living, Hakka women had to go out to work and farm.

Therefore, women had to wear the 'cooling hats' for the purpose of 'avoiding shyness', that is, they should not be seen

35th Anniversary Celebration of Wong Yuk Kong's Kwongsai Mantis

doing their work.

Almost everyone that I know or keep company with here in Pingshan Town is Hakka. Many came here from Mei Zhou, Guangdong, where Chu Gar Praying Mantis is prominent. They represent generations of Hakka in the area. Many of the women, still wear 'cooling hats'.

There were a number of exhaustive studies done on the migration of Hakka Cultures in the very early 1900's. Look for antique books if you have further interest in this subject. ---RDH

It is said that Southern Praying Mantis Kungfu is Hakka Mantis. To know more of this, read the books or eBooks—

Volume 2
China Mantis Reunion

Volume 3
Kwongsai / Iron Ox Interviews

Volume 4
On Monk Som Dot's Trail

Volume 5
Chu Gar Mantis Celebrations

Volume 2: China Mantis Reunion

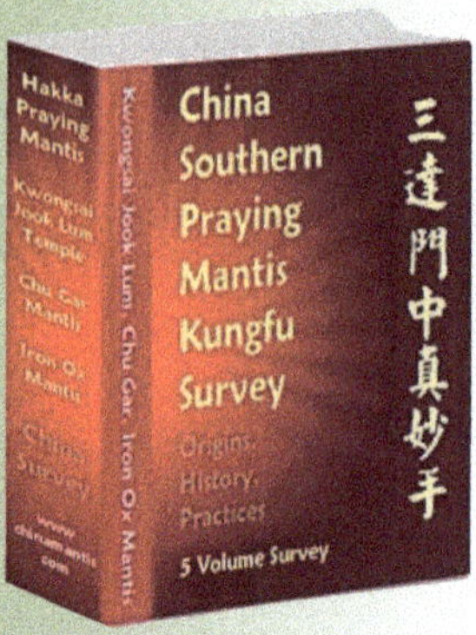

Softcover Book

or

eBook Available Now!

This Book is Volume One Pingshan Mantis Celebration

In Volume Two:

At the request of Sifu Wong Yu Hua , a number of junior, senior and elder Southern Mantis masters, dating back to circa 1920's, gathered in Huizhou, Guangdong. It's about an hour's drive from Pingshan Town and most of the mantis brothers there, had not seen each other for many years.

The gathering included those who in the 1930's and 40's, were among the in-crowd of Chu Gar and Iron Ox, as well as, Kwongsai Mantis. Some had studied all three branches of Som Dot's teaching. Learn directly from them and see their demonstrations of boxing and staff play in Volume Two of the China Southern Praying Mantis Survey.

Get your copy today!

竹林寺螳螂派

三達門中傳妙手

竹林寺內煉精功

Acknowledgements

Special thanks to Sifu Wong Yu Hua, who obviously is his father's son.

Without his friendship and invaluable assistance this ongoing China project, China Southern Praying Mantis Kungfu Survey, could not have come to pass.
Thank you.

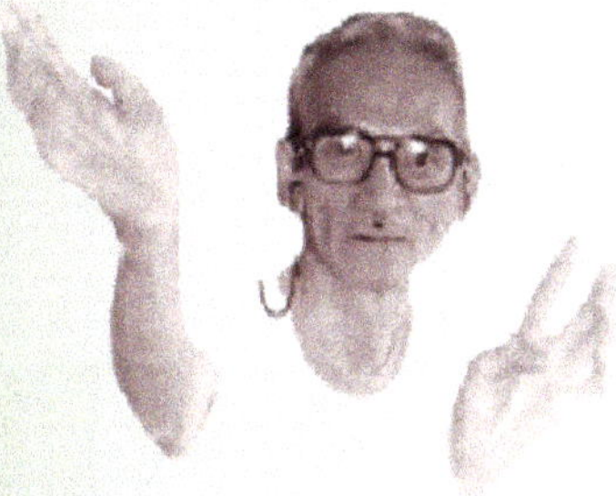

And I'll never forget too, my friendship and every Monday conversations with the late Sibok Harry Sun. He urged me onward to do this work. Rest In Peace.

So mote it be, all brothers.

Volume 3: Iron Ox / Kwongsai Mantis Interviews

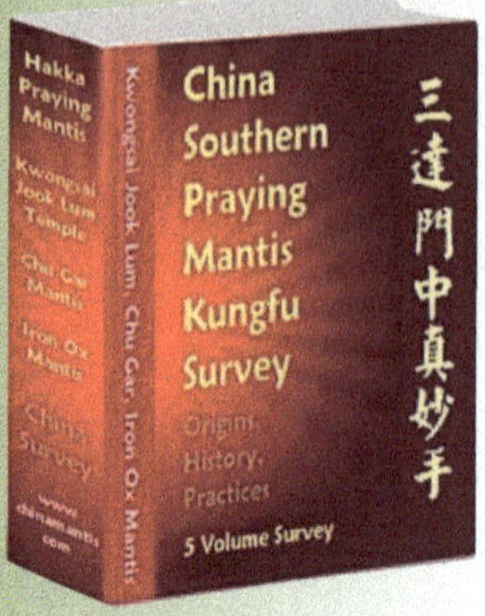

Softcover Book

or

eBook Available Now!

This Book is Volume One
Pingshan Mantis Celebration

In Volume Three:

Learn from Kwongsai Elder Master, Yao Kam Fat, who visited Lao Sui with Wong Yuk Kong. Watch his demonstrations of Third Door, Push Hands, and Plum Flower Pole Form. Hear stories which shed a great deal of light on Chung Yel Chong and Lao Sui's relationship, and other mantis ancestors.

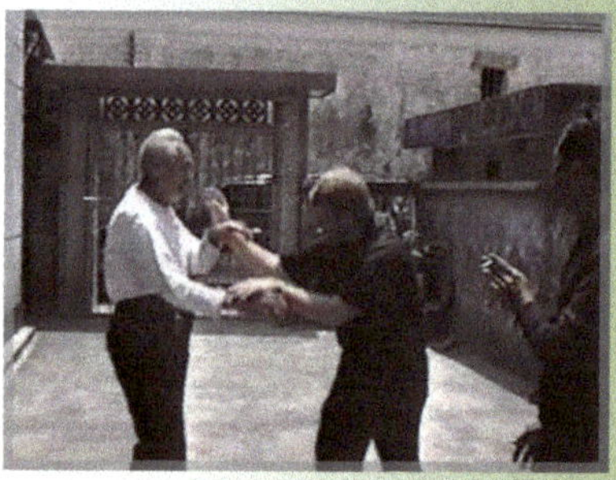

Also, Iron Uncle Chung sheds light on mantis in the very earliest days circa 1920's.

Yang Gun Ming's family interview shows the degree that mantis once permeated south China villages.

And you will discover the origin of China's Iron Ox Praying Mantis and visit with an inheritor, Sifu Xu Men Fei, as he takes you on a tour of Pingdi, an Iron Ox Village and its ancient Clan Temple. Watch demonstrations of the Iron Ox forms Second Door, Third Door, and Big Red Pole forms! Get your copy today.

Appendices

Appendix A: Wong Yu Hua Sifu Interviews

Two interviews of Sifu Wong Yu Hua. He is the son of the late Kwongsai Mantis Grandmaster Wong Yuk Kong and is considered the heir of Kwongsai Mantis in China. I have received these questions from numerous people in numerous countries, over a number of years, who requested these interviews. And so, I asked him.

Appendix B: Wong Yuk Kong's Mantis Creed

Wong Sifu opened numerous Kwongsai Mantis Schools in Hong Kong and China. Read a translation of the true heritage of his Praying Mantis Fitness Society's rules and regulations. View his 1962 Creed and see who was present in the photography. An abridged genealogy is included.

Appendix C: Wong Yu Hua's Reliquary Photographs

View rare and never before published historical photographs from the 1950's onward of Wong Yuk Kong's Schools, teaching, Fitness Society and Associations.

Appendix D: Monk Lee Siem's Dit Da Cu Formula

According to Lee Siem Yuen, Kwongsai Mantis isn't mantis without this herbal formula. It contains some 47 ingredients that can only be found at specific times on certain mountains in South China. But, even if you had all the ingredients it would be of no benefit without the refining procedure. And this is a vinegar based medicine (Dit Da Cu), not alcohol, because Lee was Buddhist!

Appendix E: Pingshan Hakka Mantis Feast

Once a year, in the Spring time, Wong Yu Hua Sifu, being Hakka, obtains a small yellow calf that has grazed only on Mountain grass and gathers friends and family at a lakeside villa for a feast of beef! Warning! This article contains graphic images!

SIFU WONG YU HUA INTERVIEWS

June, 2005, Pingshan Town, China

The following is an interview of Sifu Wong Yu Hua. He is the son of the late Kwongsai Mantis Grandmaster Wong Yuk Kong and is considered the heir of Kwongsai Mantis in China. I have received these questions from numerous people in various countries, over a number of years, who requested this interview. And so, in June 2005, I asked him:

RDH: Can you tell us what is your relationship with Henry Poo Yee from the United States?
WYH: I am not concerned with politics. There is no head of mantis only heirs. I don't make any claims except to be my father's son. I do not know Henry Yee. You know that Yee accompanied you (RDH) and Bill Chan once to Pingshan, about 1992, for a couple of days to visit me. I have only met this person that one time, thirteen years ago or more, for a day or two.

I heard in Hong Kong that Henry Yee has also stated that he is my good friend and in the past learned from my father, Wong Yuk Kong and my father's Grand Teacher, Lee Siem Si. None of this is true. It is absolutely false.

I was also told that Henry Yee came to Hong Kong and stated among the Kungfu community that he once came to see my father, accompanied by Lam Sang. None of this is true. I have contacted the media, magazines and newspapers in Hong Kong not long ago to alert them about his erroneous statements. I wish to publish an article to state the true facts. Henry Yee is not my friend, I don't know him, neither did he visit, ever see, especially, never learn from my father or my father's Teachers. One should not distort the facts for personal gain.

RDH: What do you think about Henry Yee's Mantis?
WYH: From the very little I have seen and that he showed to me, it is definitely not the Kwongsai Mantis Heritage I, my father, or my father's Teachers have received. There is no one in China who trains any of Som Dot's branches the way Henry Yee does.

RDH: Do you think Henry Yee is teaching Lam Sang's Mantis?
WYH: You know that it is difficult to translate Hakka to Mandarin, much more so, English. Lam Sang's students misinterpreted his Hakka dialect, perhaps. "Som Bo Gin" means three steps; three scissors in China. That's all. Lam Sang was a local. You have heard many stories about him. He studied Chu Gar Mantis and KwongSai Mantis. Lam Sang was a controversial figure. But, Henry Yee's Mantis does not conform to any standard in China.

RDH: Is there a Lee Pai Mantis in China from Lee Ying Sing?
WYH: No. There is no such thing. You know that. You have travelled from Hong Kong and Macau in the South to Kwongsai and to Shanxi in the North. There is no Lee Ying Sing Pai in China. Lee Ying Sing was not my father's student, although, Lee did have a brief relationship with Chung Yel Chong. But that relationship ended very early on.

RDH: Explain further please?
WYH: Lee Ying Sing, as a student of Chung Yel Chong, stirred up trouble sometimes that he couldn't extricate from himself. Unable to get out of it, on occasion, my father had to bail Lee out. Among other incidences (outside of mantis and not to be mentioned), he stirred up trouble with (the late) Wong Tam Gong, Chung Yel Chong's well respected student in Hong Kong (refer to the 1962 Praying Mantis Fitness Society Celebration in the Survey). That's why he left for England. Chung Yel Chong's students are still here and Wong Tam Gong's students are still teaching in Hong Kong. I am not one to speak ill. These are the iron facts and should not be changed or distorted to suit one's personal interest.

Appendices

RDH: Recently, there were 3 photos of your father posted on a website by Koo Kwai in Seattle, USA. Do you know him?
WYH: I don't. It is known that he was a student of my father. You have at least one photo of him and my father, that I gave you several years ago. However, his recent internet photos that I have seen, do not reflect the Mantis principle of "hands never rise above the eyebrows or fall below the knees."

My father followed his teacher, Chung Yel Chong, for seventeen years. He had numerous schools in China and Hong Kong and literally more than a thousand students. I appeal to all Tanglang disciples to love and respect the history and blossom the art. These are the iron facts about Tanglang and shouldn't be changed or made up to suit one's self or purpose.

RDH: These people that we've spoken of today, and others, outside of China, say "Red Brow or Yellow Brow" was the founder of our Art in China. What say you?
WYH: You've been in China, north to south, for a long time. Did you ever hear anyone in anyplace say so? There is no such person. This is a case of one person speaking erroneously, fictiously and everyone else then repeating it.

RDH: You've given me your father's Training manifesto from the Hong Kong schools circa. 1962, what about the teaching today?
WYH: Over time one should train at least this:

Dan Zhuang Fut Sao - Single Arm Buddha Hand
Shuang Zhuang Fut Sao - Double Arm Buddha Hand
San Bu Jian - Three Steps Three Scissors
Say Men - Four Doors
San Jian Yao Shou (Fo Bu Jian)
Ba Men - Eight *Doors*
Mui Fa Chuan - Plum Flower Fist; Forms 1-2

Appendices

Tanglang Darn Dao - Single and Double Broadsword
Tanglang Jian - Mantis Single and Double Straight Sword
Chien Wu Jian - Straight Piercing Sword
Hou Wu Jian - Backward Piercing Sword
Say Men Gun - Four Doors Wooden Staff
Mui Fa Gun - Plum Flower Wooden Staff
Tanglang Kwan Dao - Mantis Long Handled Broadsword
Tanglang Tieh Cha - Mantis Iron Rulers (sai)
Tanglang Sha Dao -
Tanglang Wu Xing - Mantis 5 Rope Dart
Tanglang Ying Chiang - Mantis Iron Spear
Tanglang Fu Dao - Mantis Tiger Fork
Tanglang Ji - A unique wood and iron straight long weapon

RDH: Can you sum it up in a few words?
WYH: It is like this:
TUN - Float (the body)
TO - Spit (the body)
TU - Spring Power
YAO - Soft Power
JIAN - Cut like scissors

The hands never go above the eyebrows;
Never fall below the knees.
Certainly this is not all, only a summation.

My father, Wong Yuk Kong, was 14 when he began in 1930 to learn from his Teacher, Chung Yel Chong. He followed him for 17 years from 1930 to 1947. My father passed when he was 52 years old in 1968.

The photo below was of one of my father's schools in Shatoujow. (Wong shown centered in gray suit). Yeung Yan sits to my father's right as you look. Yeung Yan, after learning mantis from my father, early on went to teach Mantis in England.

Appendices

His teaching was standard and his student's today still retain the Kwongsai Mantis' root and art in the UK.

This photo, circa 1960, made off the southern coast at a village in Guangdong Province states:

Upper Grain Threshing Floor Village
Mr. Li's Allied Hero Society
Allied Hero Society's Unicorn Brought to Light
By the Seal of Authority --Months, -- Years

Student shirts read: Allied Hero Society

Yeung Yan's shirt reads:
Praying Mantis Fitness Society Clan 102

Appendices

Second Interview

Autumn 2005, Pingshan Town

RDH: When did your father go to Malaysia?
WYH: At age 19, my father went to Malaysia, along with other local people. Times were difficult and they all sought food and work. He found labor on a 'junk', a Chinese boat. There were many Kungfu men working on the boats in Malaysia, predominantly Chinese, too.

When the daily work was done, everyone always drank wine and ate together, on the boats. One night, there were too many men, on the boat, and one person took exception to my father, fearing that he might lose his job to my father's efforts. So, that person, soon, sought a priest to place an incantation, a spell, upon my father.

Later, my father returned home, to China, and settled in Huidong. But, it seems the spell, may have been of effect. He climbed up five stories on the corner of a building. His first wife's account states that he truly looked like an insect, able to climb up walls five stories tall, at once.

Many local people asked him to come down, but he wouldn't listen. It was only when his Sifu, Cheng Yel Chong, came and commanded him to come down, that he immediately scaled the wall back down, in the same way he had gone up.

It was said that he was fearful of his teacher, Chung Yel Chong, who quickly went to a local temple and used his own incantations to speed Wong Yuk Kong's recovery. Witnesses say that after Master Chung's chants, three black worms, about three inches long, emerged from the crown of Wong Yuk Kong's (bai hui-hundred meeting points) head.

Appendices

Afterwards, Wong Yuk Kong returned to himself and continued his teachings to many students. My father's first wife, at the time, attested that she saw the whole affair.

Everyone called my father, Wong Yuk Kong, Uncle Rock, because his body could withstand punches and kicks without harm, due to his continual mantis training which strengthens the bones and hardens the sinews.

RDH: How did your father meet his teacher, Chung Yel Chong?
WYH: At an early age, Chung Yel Chong sought students at an opium den in Pingshan village. Chung Wu Xing, who I introduced you to some years ago, was Chung's Yel Chong's first student.

Everyone also called Chung Wu Xing, Iron Bok - Iron Uncle, for the same reason they did my father. You interviewed Iron Uncle several years ago when he was in his mid 90's. He has passed on now. He said students gave sacks of rice or staples to learn mantis instead of giving money, when there wasn't any money to give. The students in those very early years gave their wholehearted interest, their soul.

RDH: I appreciate that you (in the past and now) still look and care for those Kwongsai Mantis brothers, uncles, and your father's friends, students and teachers. What about your father's introduction to Chung Yel Chong? How did he become Chung Yel Chong's student?

WYH: At that time, in the 1920's or so, in my uncle's opium den, Cheng Yel Chong divided students into groups and secretly taught them Kwongsai Mantis.

One day, as a teenager, my father was caught by Chung Yel

Appendices

Chong, inside, practicing Mantis. He had been secretly watching from the outside wall every day, and exercising himself. Immediately, Master Chung caught my father, the young Wong, by the shoulder and asked, "Who is this boy"?

Afterwards, Master Chung took my father, as a young boy, to be his apprentice and for 17 years he followed Master Chung until his death.

L-R) Wong Yuk Kong's Sister, Wong Yuk Kong's Son (Wong Yu Hua), and his mother, Wong Yuk Kong's Wife, 2007 New Year

To know more about Master Chung's life and death, read Volume 4; On Som Dot's Trail.

To learn what Kwongsai Jook Lum Mantis Wong Yuk Kong Sifu passed down, read on in Appendix B.

1962 Hong Kong Praying Mantis Fitness Society

Bamboo Forest Temple True Heritage

Sifu Wong Yuk Kong's Rules and Regulations

Chinese Doctor, Wong Yuk Kong
Illnesses Diagnosed

Treatments include
Spiritual Work
Internal and External Herbal Formulas

1. Carry on the National Art (Guo Shu - Martial Art) with a tradition of hard work and plain living, exercising daily to build up a strong and robust physique with Spirit in the bones.

2. No discrimination; young and old, male and female may become a member. Ordinary people may correct their thinking while refining their health, morals, actions, behavior and conduct to become righteous,
upright and regular.

Enter your name by the registrar and abide by the Founder's intention, abide by the rules and regulations.

3A. School Curriculum; Primary Stage:
Horse stance
Single Arm Form
Two Arms Form
Three Scissors-
Shaking* Bridge Form
(*Shake, wave, rock, turn, wag)
Four Doors Fist Form
Flexible Fists and Feet Form

Appendix B contains a translation of the pamphlet distributed by Wong Yuk Kong Sifu's Hakka Mantis Society. Also, refer to Appendix D, Historical Photographs of this Society.

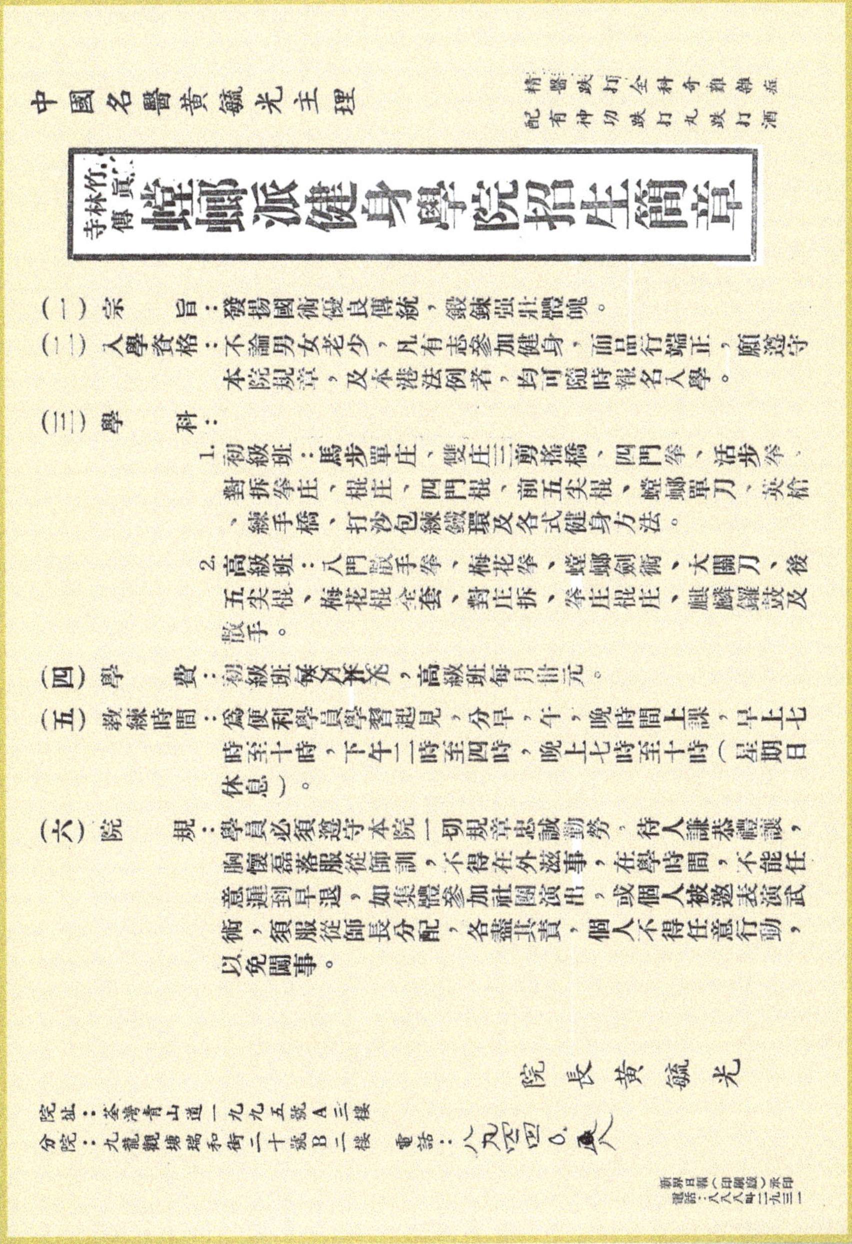

中國名醫黃毓光主理

精醫跌打全科奇難雜症
配有神功跌打丸跌打酒

少林竹林寺真傳

螳螂派健身學院招生簡章

（一）宗　旨：發揚國術優良傳統，鍛鍊強壯體魄。

（二）入學資格：不論男女老少，凡有志參加健身，而品行端正，願遵守本院規章，及本港法例者，均可隨時報名入學。

（三）學　科：

1. 初級班：馬步單庄、雙庄三箭搖橋、四門拳、活步拳、對拆拳庄、棍庄、四門棍、前五尖棍、螳螂單刀、英槍、練手橋、打沙包練鐵環及各式健身方法。

2. 高級班：八門散手拳、梅花拳、螳螂劍術、大關刀、後五尖棍、梅花棍全套、對庄拆、拳庄棍庄、麒麟鑼鼓及散手。

（四）學　費：初級班每月[illegible]元，高級班每月卅元。

（五）教練時間：爲便利學員學習起見，分早，午，晚時間上課，早上七時至十時，下午二時至四時，晚上七時至十時（星期日休息）。

（六）院　規：學員必須遵守本院一切規章忠誠勤勞，待人謙恭禮讓，胸懷磊落服從師訓，不得在外滋事，在學時間，不能任意遲到早退，如集體參加社團演出，或個人被邀表演武術，須服從師長分配，各盡其責，個人不得任意行動，以免闖事。

院長黃毓光

院址：荃灣青山道一九九五號A三樓
分院：九龍觀塘瑞和街二十號B二樓　電話：八九四四0八

新界日報(印刷廠)承印 電話：八八八四二九三一

1962 Hong Kong Praying Mantis Fitness Society

Bamboo Forest Temple True Heritage

Sifu Wong Yuk Kong's Rules and Regulations

Counter-dismantle Fist Wood Pole
Wooden Staff
Four Doors Staff
Five Forward Piercing Staff
Praying Mantis Single Broadsword
Hero Spear Form
Refining the Bridge Form
Strike a Sandbag Form
Iron Circle Apparatus Form
Uncommon Form Method

3B. Senior Rank Class:
Eight Doors Fighting Form
Plum Flower Form
Praying Mantis Sword Form
Close Big Door Broadsword
Five Backward Piercing Staff
Plum Flower Staff Complete Set
Tear Open With No Reply Wood Form
Fist and Staff Wood Form
Unicorn Dance / Competition

4. Tuition:
Primary and Senior Rank
Students are required to pay monthly tuition.

5. School Hours: Monday thru Saturday
Morning 7 - 10 am
Afternoon 2- 4 pm
Evening 7 - 10 pm
Sunday - Day of Rest

Sifu Wong Yuk Kong's 1962 Kwongsai Praying Mantis Fitness Society Celebration

Centered left of the 'Unicorn' and in VIP position is Kwongsai Jook Lum Master, Wong Yuk Kong (badge on lapel). To his left is Chu Kwong Hua (Lao Sui's inheritor), friends Lok and You (Bok Mei Pai) and a local government official. To his right is Wang Tam Gong (Chung Yel Chong's Student), Chu Kwong Fang (Chu Kwong Hua's Brother), Chen Kong Hai, Yip Sui (in Chinese dress) and Liu Kwok Dong (Iron Ox Pai). The photo truly speaks a thousand words.

Can you name the Chu Gar, 'Chow Gar', Iron Ox and Bak Mei Sifu who were friends?

1962 Hong Kong Praying Mantis Fitness Society

Bamboo Forest Temple True Heritage

Sifu Wong Yuk Kong's Rules and Regulations

6. Regulations:

Do not cheat others;
Do not be lazy or neglect your responsibilities;
Be courteous and thoughtful of others;
Have lofty aspirations and high ideals;
Be openhearted and upright;
Respect the teacher and follow his instructions to the detail;
Do not create (outside) a (public) disturbance or stir up trouble;
Come to the school regularly;
Be prompt and punctual always; Do not be late for classes;
If the School takes part in public activities or celebrations, participation is mandatory;
One member may go, if invited to demonstrate Kungfu;
Accept any Job the Teacher assigns within the organization, each according to his ability and talent;
Individuals must work within the collective spirit for the benefit of the whole group;
Check carefully to avoid mistakes thus bringing shame to yourself and disaster to the organization;
Settle all affairs in the right way.

Headmaster Wong Yuk Kong, 1962

Locations:
Hong Kong
Tsuen Wan
Kowloon Tong

XINZAI RIBAO YUANSHUA CHANG CHENYING
(The Brochure's Printing Company Name)

1962 Hong Kong Praying Mantis Fitness Society

Bamboo Forest Temple True Heritage

Kwongsai Jook Lum Temple Mantis Genealogy*

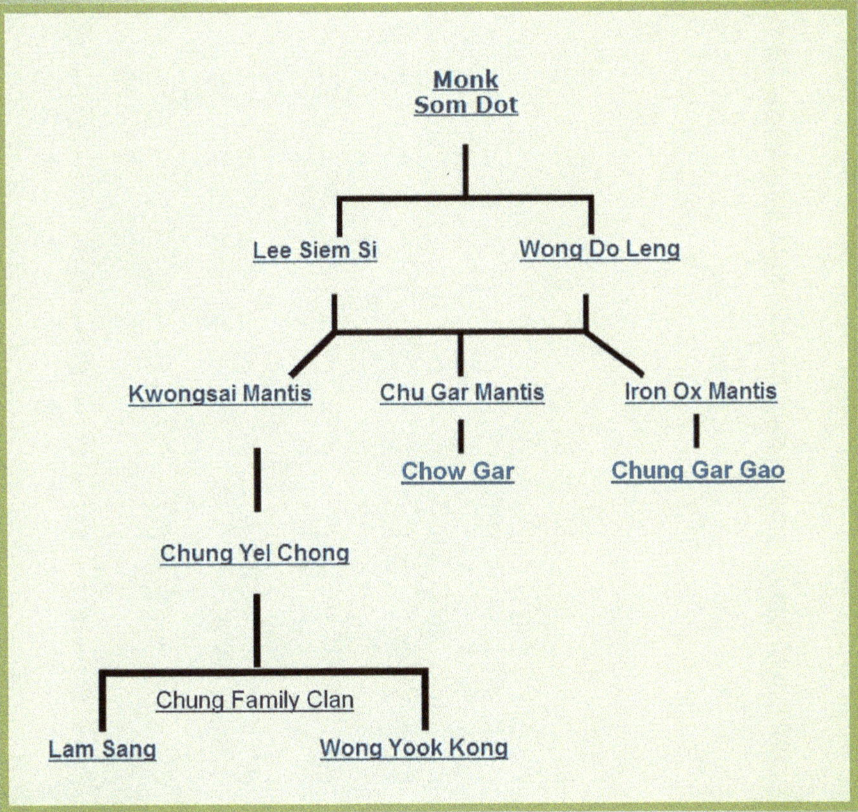

Our Ancestral Record*

"Without a standard to follow there is no root,
Without a root the tree cannot blossom.
A false standard breeds a false teaching and art." ...Hakka Maxim

*As recorded in China. Apologies to Brother-Friends of the same Clan worldwide not listed. Future publications will include further details including Chu Gar and Iron Ox.

Historical Photographs

Wong Yuk Kong, Fourth Generation, Kwongsai Mantis

Bamboo Forest Temple True Heritage

Wong Yuk Kong seated center with lapel badge. Yip Sui, Chinese dress, to Wong's right.
Wong's 1962 Hong Kong Praying Mantis Fitness Society. Refer to page 69.

Historical Photographs

Wong Yuk Kong seated center in white. Chung Yel Chong's student Wong Tam Gong, Zhang Gun Hai—Producer Wong Fei Hong movie, Yeung Yam and others. 1963 Mantis Fitness Society.

Bamboo Forest Temple True Heritage

Wong Yuk Kong seated left in white shirt. Wong Tam Gong, Zhang Gun Hai, Yeung Yam (UK), kneeling, and others. Wong's Hong Kong Mantis Fitness Society. Shatoujiao—coastal village.

Historical Photographs

Wong Yuk Kong, center. Chung Yel Chong's student Wong Tam Gong, Zhang Gun Hai—Producer Wong Fei Hong, Yeung Yam (UK), Liu Kok Dong (Iron Ox) and others.
Wong's Hong Kong Praying Mantis Fitness Society, circa 1960.

Bamboo Forest Temple True Heritage

Wong Yuk Kong, center, behind the Unicorn. To his left, Zhang Gun Hoi—producer of the Wong Fei Hong vs. Jook Lum Temple movie. Wong lives up to his creed as shown in this circa 60's photo and teaches two female students. Novel for his day!

Historical Photographs

Wong Yuk Kong Sifu literally had more than one thousand students (and some disciples) before his passing in 1968. Shown is Yeung Yam's clan before Yeung moved and taught others in England.

Bamboo Forest Temple True Heritage

Wong Yuk Kong's son, Wong Yu Hua, has carried forward his father's teaching and was recognized by the government in 2009 for his contribution to China's Intangible Cultural Heritage.

Front gate to his reliquary-"Guang Wu Tang"

Historical Photographs

After Wong Yuk Kong's passing in 1968, his students carried forward his teaching as can be seen in this 1973 photo of their Assn. dedicated to him. His teaching continues in 2012, Pingshan, China.

Bamboo Forest Temple True Heritage

Wong Yu Hua Sifu, center, has carried forward and blossomed even further his father's transmission and heritage. 2012, Pingshan Town, he teaches both Unicorn and the Hakka Mantis Boxing.

To hear what Jook Lum Temple medicine was passed down, read Appendix D.

Bamboo Forest Temple True Heritage Prescription

Kwongsai Dragon Tiger Mountain Dit Da Jow

According to Lee Siem Yuen, Kwongsai Mantis isn't Mantis without this herbal formula. It contains some 47 ingredients that can only be found at specific times on certain mountains. Try asking your local Chinese pharmacist to fill this prescription. If he can, please let me know.

But, even if you had all the ingredients it would be of no benefit without the refining procedure. And this is a vinegar based medicine (Dit Da Cu), not alcohol (Monk Lee was Buddhist). It requires 100 days of preparation and then a full moon and overnight repeated process like Zhang Daoling refining an elixir of immortality. I've made a batch (about 30 gallons) with Sifu Wong Yu Hua and the only difference is the dragon and tiger don't show up in the clouds!

I also use this when needed and it works. The only side effect is that my fair skin sometimes is left with a slight rash. I present this for your consideration only. The label shown goes on the bottles of jow given or sold to Sifu Wong's patients.

The Medical Clinic of Sifu Wong Yu Hua, son of the late Kwongsai Mantis Grandmaster, Wong Yuk Kong, treats patients regularly in Pingshan Town today using Som Dot's prescriptions. I have accompanied him to treat the elderly (which he often does free of charge).

The Clinic's outer sign states -

Kwongsai Jook Lum Temple
Teaching True Praying Mantis Boxing.
Dit Da Zhong Yi - Doctor of Traditional Chinese Medicine—
Wong Yu Hua.

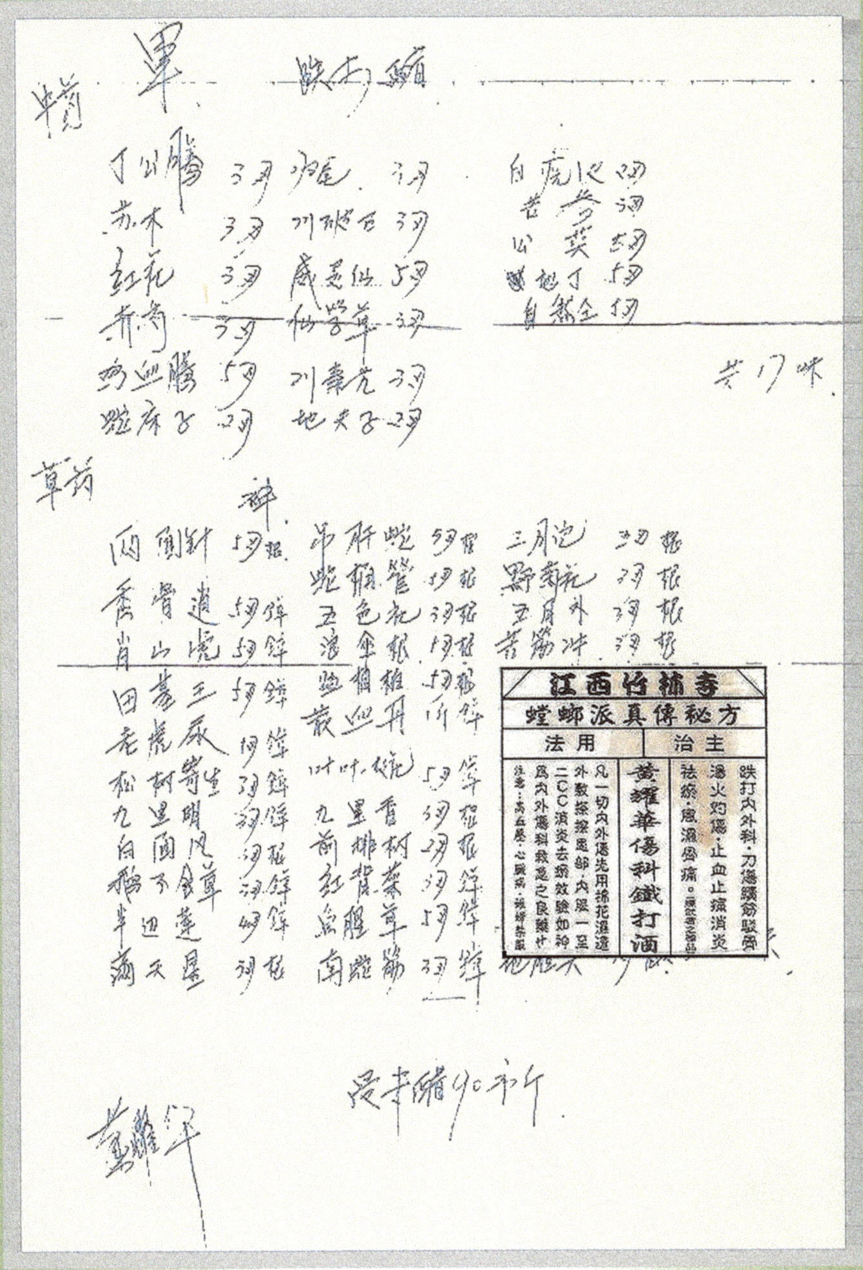

To join a Hakka Feast in
Pingshan, the hometown of Kwongsai Mantis, read on.

Warning! This appendix contains graphic images.

Join a Hakka Feast in Pingshan, Hometown of Kwongsai Jook Lum Mantis

Once a year, in the Spring time, Wong Yu Hua Sifu, being Hakka, obtains a small yellow calf that has grazed only on Mountain grass and gathers family and friends at a lakeside villa for a feast of beef!

The little calf doesn't suffer but for those who buy their food in the supermarket, it may seem cruel (at first). I have to admit the little calf did seem to look up at me as if to say, "help!"

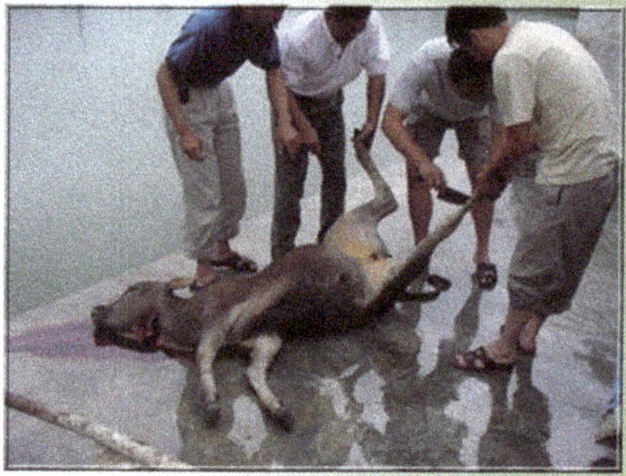

Of course, when in Rome you do as the Romans, and I was guest of honor at this Hakka feast and did not wish to impose on my most gracious Hakka Chinese host, the western supermarket hunter / gatherer's idea of how to obtain beef! Although, I did decline to join in the butchering.

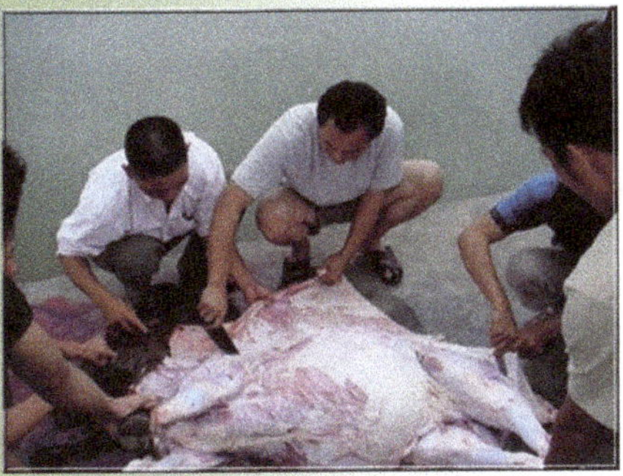

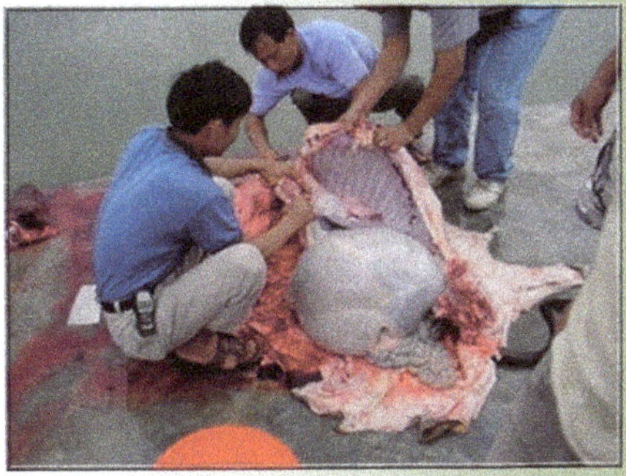

Taken down to the lakeside, the calf is first knocked completely unconscious with a sledgehammer right between the eyes.

Then, its throat is cut and it is allowed to bleed out until dead. A quick examination of its eyes make that determination.

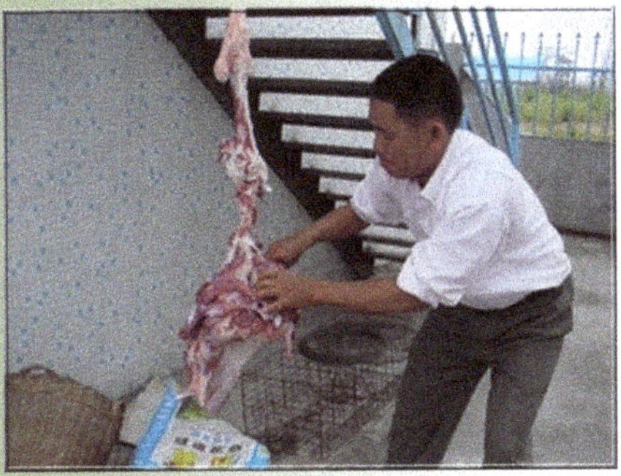

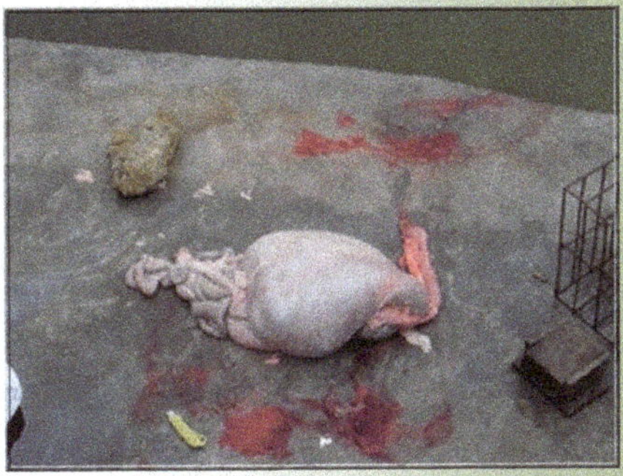

After it is clear that the animal is dead, its head is cut off and discarded into the lake. I couldn't help but wonder how many cow heads (or otherwise) laid in the water at the bottom of that concrete slab?

At this point all the men join in with the meat cleavers and beginning with the legs skin the calf completely. With great dexterity and obvious experience in a matter of just minutes the cow's hide is completely removed.

The meat is then removed from the bone with the skill of master butchers. Some is hung up and cubed, some is made to into beef stew, some into deep fried beef steaks and in all some dozen

Join a Hakka Feast in Pingshan, Hometown of Kwongsai Jook Lum Mantis

dishes are made until there is absolutely nothing gone to waste. The only thing remaining of the little yellow calf was his intestinal tract and stomach sac!

L) Wong Sifu, Wong Simu and RDH; R) Guests of the Hakka Feast!

When it was time to enjoy the feast, and after tasting the delectable beef dishes (I usually don't eat beef), I stated the only reason Buddha didn't eat beef was because no one treated him to a Hakka feast!

To discover more
Hakka Southern Mantis resources,
online and off,
read the following pages.

Volume 4: On Som Dot's Trail / Chung Family Interviews

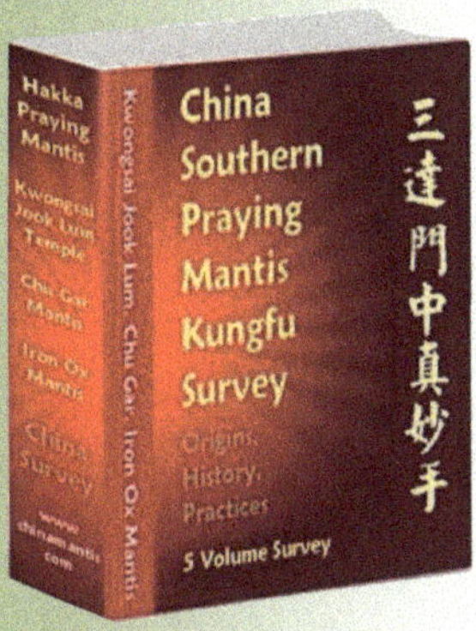

Softcover Book
or
eBook Available Now!

This Book is Volume One Pingshan Mantis Celebration

In Volume Four:

INTERVIEWS

Visit Chung Yel Chong's (Zhang Yaozong), third Ancestor's, family and clinic and watch his grandson perform treatments; an in-depth interview of Chung Yel Chong's family. Rare photographs.

An interview with Sifu Lee Kwok Liang in Hong Kong, who was a student of Kwongsai Mantis Masters Chang Gun Hoi and Wong Yuk Kong. Lee Sifu still teaches in Hong Kong today and his son, Patrick is a mantis Sifu, as well.

ON SOM DOT'S TRAIL

Visit Shanxi in the North and Jiangxi (Kwongsai) in the South of China where Som Dot and Lee Siem Yuen treaded. See what the old Bamboo Forest Temple located in Shanxi looks like today! And visit the bamboo forests of Mt. Dragon Tiger and the mansions of the first Taoist Pope where the "108" Demons were confined into a well.

Hear what the elders at the Macau Bamboo Forest Temple had to say about Lee Siem Yuen! And more. Get your copy today!

Resources

Our Family of Hakka Mantis Websites

Visit and Enjoy! Informational, Educational, Instructive

www.SouthernMantisPress.com

A ten year ongoing research in China
of the origins, history and practices of Southern Mantis!

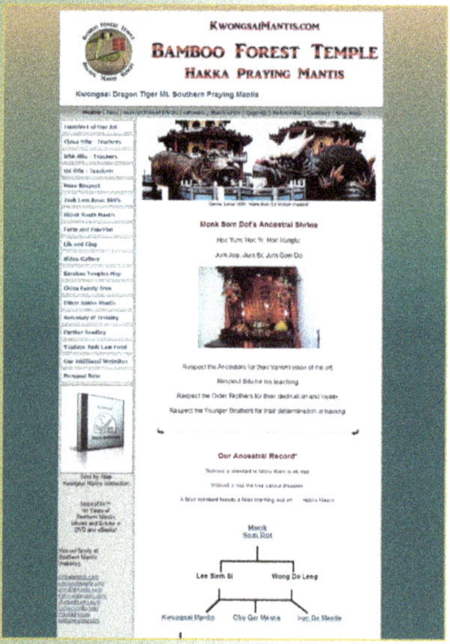

Dedicated to the late Wong Yuk Kong Sifu in China!
chinamantis.com

The Bamboo Temple Association is a mutual aid fraternity. Join us and become a member, School, Branch or Study Group to-day! Dedicated to the late Lam Sang Sifu's teaching in the USA.
bambootemple.com
bambootemple-chicago.com
btcba.com

These sites reveal many China Kwongsai Mantis Sifu who have heretofore remained silent about the teaching of Kwongsai
Dragon Tiger Mountain Bamboo Forest Temple Mantis and outlay the lineage of Hakka Mantis as stated in China.
kwongsaimantis.com
somdotmantis.com

This site details the complete history of Chu Gar Gao Hakka Praying Mantis as descended from the late Lao Sui in Hong Kong and Hui Yang (Wai Yearn), China.

Online

(con't) Dedicated to the late Cheng Wan Sifu who passed in 2009. chugarmantis.com

This site is dedicated to the late Xu Fat Chun Sifu and speaks of the history of Iron Ox Hakka Praying Mantis in Pingdi Town, Guangdong, China.
ironoxmantis.com

Historical Hakka Mantis Flix! Some 60+ years of Hakka Southern Praying Mantis Kungfu movies and events in video eBooks!
mantisflix.com

Our dedicated South Mantis Tube. We have several hundreds of hours of videos in our Hakka Mantis archives dating back to 1950 in China that we hope to share with you! Feel free to share. Upload your Southern Mantis or Hakka video now!
southmantis.com

Genuine Internal Work - the original 11 month correspondence course of Tien Tao Qigong.
tientaoqigong.com

Ancient Methods to achieve vitality and a healthier well-being! The Oriental Secrets Series of Qigong.
oss.tientaoqigong.com

And visit our daily Youtube video feed of only Southern Praying Mantis videos!
chinamantis.com/youtube

And our Youtube channel:
youtube.com/chinamantissurvey

ChinaMantis.com Instructional DVDs

Jook Lum Temple Mantis
Step by Step Instruction in 18 Volumes

Year One Training

Volume One: Fundamentals; The Most Important
Volume Two: Phoenix Eye Fist Attacking / Stepping
Volume Three: Centerline Defense
Volume Four: One, Three & Nine Step Attack / Defense
Volume Five: Centerline Sticky Hand Training
Volume Six: Same Hand / Opposite Hand Attacks
Volume Seven: Sai Shu, Sik Shu, Jik (Chun) Shu
Volume Eight: Gow Choy; Hammer Fist-Internal Strength
Volume Nine: Footwork in Southern Praying Mantis
Volume 10 Chi Sao Sticky Hands and Pass offs

Advanced Two Man Forms—Year Two and Three

Available by request. Prerequisite Volumes 1–10.

Volume 11: Loose Hands One
Volume 12: Som Bo Gin
Volume 13: Second Loose Hands
Volume 14: 108 Subset
Volume 15: Um Hon One
Volume 16: Um Hon Two
Volume 17: Mui Fa Plum Flower
Volume 18: Eighteen Buddha Hands

All 8 two man forms must be trained as one continuous set on both A - B sides.

Summary Year One

http://www.chinamantis.com/first-year-training.htm

Summary Year Three:

http://www.chinamantis.com/summary-of-training.htm

New Media from Southern Mantis Press.com

Southern Mantis Instructional Playing Cards

Kwongsai Mantis
18 Buddha Hands

Card Backs: Various Sifu of Lam Sang's generations in multiple postures

Card Fronts: Two man application photos, Text instruction, Instructive maxims

Includes the 18 Buddha Hands and more of Kwongsai Hakka Mantis

Key Benefits of our Card Decks

- 54 Cards with Hakka Mantis
- Customized Front and Back
- Full Vibrant Color!
- Instructional
- Educational
- Informative
- Rare and Exclusive Content and Photographs
- Entertaining - Play Hakka Mantis Cards with your friends

More on the following page!

New Media from Southern Mantis Press.com

Southern Mantis Instructional Playing Cards

Card Deck Use Includes

- Useful gifts for martial artists
- Instructional and Informative
- Invaluable Heirloom of Hakka Mantis Masters

Card Decks Include

- 54 card deck in standard size
- Made from 100% casino quality card stock
- Clear plastic case included

Wholesale Inquiries Welcome

Other Decks Include:

- Chu Gar Mantis - "Fundamentals"
- China Kwongsai Mantis - "Celebration"

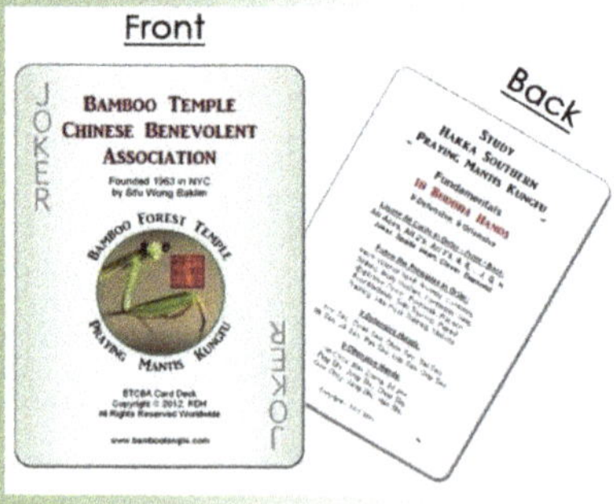

For order info email:

cards@chinamantis.com

MantisFlix™ Video eBooks

60 Years of Southern Mantis Movies and Events!

Wong Fei Hong and the Jook Lum Temple

Volume 1001 - Hong Kong 1954

B/W Classic Movie Exclusive! 100,000 plus clip previews on Youtube. Get your full copy now!

Kwongsai Mantis Celebration

Volume 1002 - Pingshan Town, Guangdong, China

Late Sifu Wong Yuk Kong Kwongsai Jook Lum Clan 35th Anniversary Celebration, circa 2003.

Hakka Boxing Collection One

Volume 1003 - A rare collection of Hakka Boxing.

Hakka Boxing Collection Two

Volume 1004 - A second rare collection of Hakka Boxing.

Chu Gar Cheng Wan Celebration

Volume 1005 - Join the 1989 Cheng Wan Chu Gar Mantis Celebration in Hong Kong! Cheng Wan Sifu was the inheritor of Chu Gar descended from Lao Sui.

View and Enjoy Video Previews Online:
www.MantisFlix.com

Join a School or Start a Study Group!

Bamboo Temple Chinese Benevolent Association

Roger D. Hagood, Standing Chairman
Hong Kong, Shenzhen, China
rdh@chinamantis.com

USA

Crystal Lake, Illinois School
Richard Lee Gamboa
USA Chief Instructor
Phone: (847) 458-2080
Mantis@ActionKungFu.com

Los Angeles, CA School
John Brown
Phone: (510) 423 1615
Tonglong108@gmail.com

Huntsville - North AL, Branch
Slade White
256-694-0949
slade@sladewhite.com

Indiana, USA Branch
Dave Marshall
812-709-0827
ictdave@aol.com

Washington DC Study Group
Eric Lewis
240-552-1338
rev_ericlewis@hotmail.com

Weslaco, TX Study Group
David Garcia
(956) 472-0254
garciads1@gmail.com

INT'L

Taipei, Taiwan Branch
Dr. Han Chih Lu
simonclh@gmail.com

London, Ontario, Canada Branch
Mike Shaw
Phone 519-852-2174
mantismike@start.ca

Düsseldorf, Germany Branch
Erik Irsch
eirsch@yahoo.de

Lima Peru Study Group
Guillermo E. Talavera
getalavera@hotmail.com

Like minded people that have a sincere interest to study Southern Praying Mantis together and are following the Instructional DVDs may start a Study Group.
Become a group leader today!

Volume 5: Chu Gar Mantis
Cheng Wan Sifu Celebrations

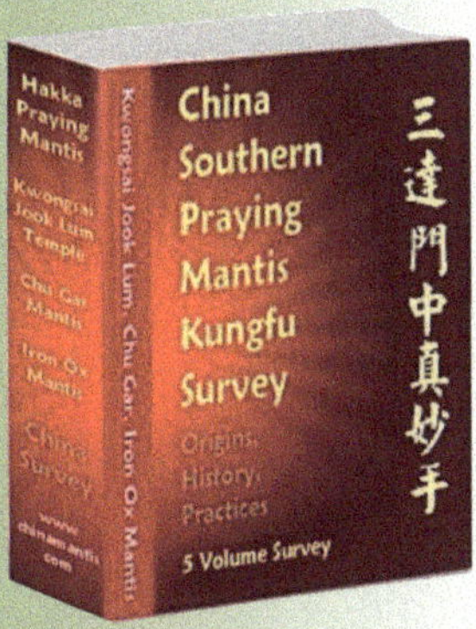

Softcover Book

or

eBook Available Now!

This Book is Volume One
Pingshan Mantis Celebration

In Volume Five:

You will discover more about the origins, history and practices of Chu Gar Praying Mantis.

I studied Chu Gar Mantis with Sifu Gene Chen, who was a disciple of Dong Yat Long, who was a disciple of Sun Chu Hing, who was a disciple of Lao Sui. I did "make the ceremony" of offering tea to Chen Sifu and so became his disciple in Chu Gar Mantis, circa 1989. I am also a disciple by Ceremony of the Late Grandmaster Cheng Wan in Hong Kong!

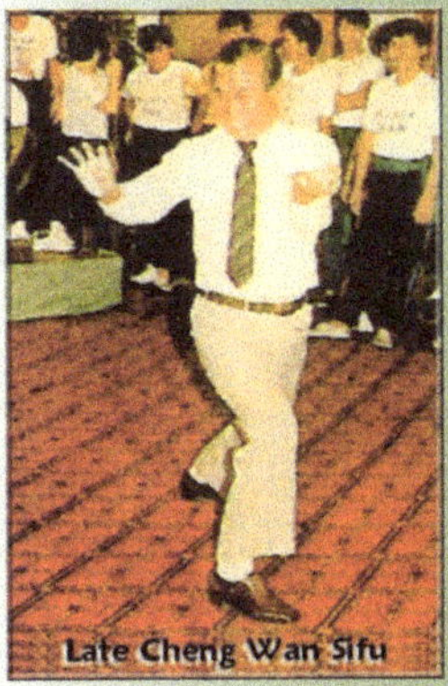
Late Cheng Wan Sifu

See performances of soft and hard power in Chu Gar boxing as well as learn the Origins, History and Practices of this rare Hakka Mantis boxing style.

Get your copy today!

RDH Bio

Welcome to visit the Author!

Your email correspondence is welcome and do visit and study Hakka Southern Praying Mantis with me in beautiful sunny south China! I am an Author, Publisher and Producer of eBooks, books, journals, videos and 7 International martial arts newsstand magazines in 15 countries with 44 years in training and teaching martial arts and some 20 years living in China and Asia!

Currently residing in beautiful sunny south China for the last 10 years. Join my class in Guangdong today!

RDH
Pingshan Town
Summer 2012

More Bio:

http://www.chinamantis.com/roger-d.-hagood.htm

Email:

rdh@chinamantis.com

Guang Wu Tang
Study Hakka Mantis and Unicorn in China
Jook Lum Temple Mantis and Hakka Unicorn Culture
Study in
Beautiful South China!
Train Hakka Unicorn Culture at
Guang Wu Tang—The Martial Hall
of Wong Yuk Kong!
Sifu Wong Yu Hua
Pingshan Town
for info email:
rdh@chinamantis.com

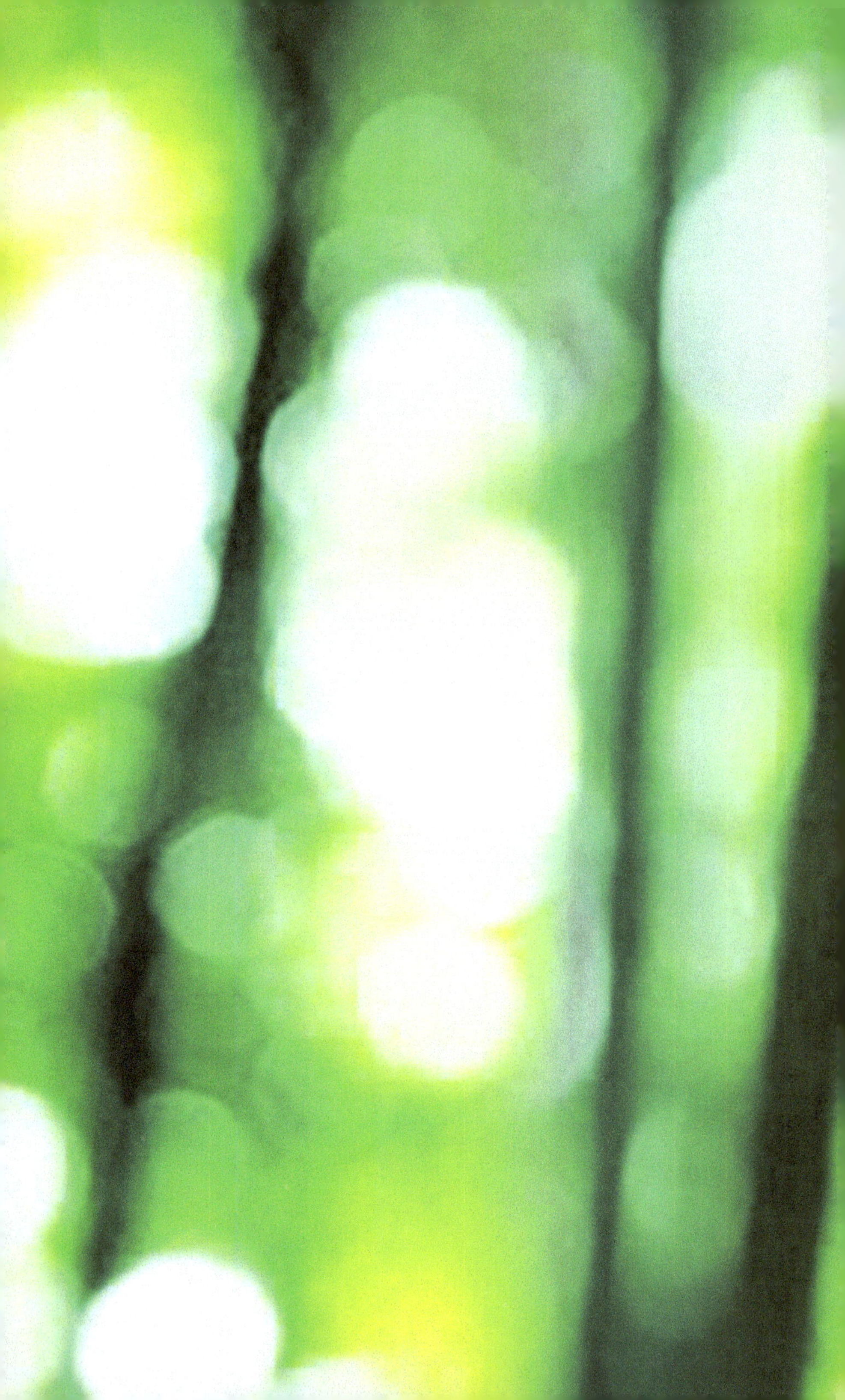

www.ingramcontent.com/pod-product-compliance
Lightning Source LLC
Chambersburg PA
CBHW040406110426
42812CB00011B/2469
9780985724009